A Student in Arms

DONALD HANKEY

New York 1917

TABLE OF CONTENTS

SOMETHING ABOUT A STUDENT IN ARMS
AUTHOR'S FOREWORD
THE POTENTATE
THE BAD SIDE OF MILITARY SERVICE
THE GOOD SIDE OF MILITARISM
A MONTH'S REFLECTIONS
ROMANCE
IMAGINARY CONVERSATIONS
THE FEAR OF DEATH IN WAR
IMAGINARY CONVERSATIONS
THE WISDOM OF A STUDENT IN ARMS
IMAGINARY CONVERSATIONS
LETTER TO AN ARMY CHAPLAIN
DON'T WORRY
IMAGINARY CONVERSATIONS
A PASSING IN JUNE 1915
MY HOME AND SCHOOL
CHAPTER I. MY HOME
CHAPTER II. SCHOOL
SOME NOTES ON THE FRAGMENT OF
AUTOBIOGRAPHY BY HILDA

SOMETHING ABOUT A STUDENT IN ARMS

By H.M.A.H.

"His life was a Romance of the most noble and beautiful kind." So says one who has known him from childhood, and into how many dull, hard and narrow lives has he not been the first to bring the element of Romance?

He carried it about with him; it breathes through his writings, and this inevitable expression of it gives the saying of one of his friends, that "it is as an artist that we shall miss him most," the more significance.

And does not the artist as well as the poet live forever in his works? Is not the breath of inspiration that such alone can breathe into the dull clods of their generation bound to be immortal?

Meanwhile, his "Romance" is to be written and his biographer will be one whose good fortune it has been to see much of the "Student" in Bermondsey, the place that was the forcing-house of his development. In the following pages it is proposed only to give an outline of his life, and particularly the earlier and therefore to the public unknown parts.

Donald Hankey was born at Brighton in 1884; he was the seventh child of his parents, and was welcomed with excitement and delight by a ready-made family of three brothers and two sisters living on his arrival amongst them. He was the youngest of them by seven years, and all had their plans for his education and future, and waited jealously for the time when he should be old enough to be removed from the loving shelter of his mother's arms and be "brought up."

His education did, as a matter of fact,begin at a very early age; for one day, when he was perhaps about three years old, dressed in a white woolly cap and coat, and out for his morning walk, a neighbouring baby stepped across from his nurse's side and with one well-directed blow felled Donald to the ground! Donald was too much astonished and hurt at the sheer injustice of the assault to dream of retaliation, but when they reached home and his indignant nurse told the story, he was taken aside by his brothers and made to understand that by his failure to resist the assault, and give the other fellow back as good as he gave, "the honour of the family" was impugned! He was then and there put through a systematic course of "the noble art of self-defence." "And I think," said one of his brothers only the other day, "that he was prepared to act upon his instructions should occasion arise." It will be seen from this incident that his bringing-up was of a decidedly strenuouscharacter and likely to make Donald's outlook on life a serious one!

He was naturally a peace-loving and philosophical little boy, very lovable and attractive with his large clear eyes with their curious distribution of colour—the one entirely blue and the other three parts a decided brown—the big head set proudly on the slender little body, and the radiant illuminating smile, that no one who knew him well at any time of his life can ever forget. It spoke of a light within, "that mysterious light which is of course not physical," as was said by one who met him only once, but was quick to note this characteristic.

Donald's more strenuous times were in the boys' holidays—those tumultuous of seasons so well known to the members of all big families! His eldest brother, Hugh, was bent on making an all-round athlete of him; another brother saw in him an embryo county cricketer, while a third was mostparticular about his music, giving him lessons on the violoncello with clockwork regularity. The games were terribly thrilling and dangerous, especially when the schoolroom was turned into a miniature battlefield, with opposing armies of tiny lead soldiers. But Donald never turned a hair if Hugh were present, even at the most terrific explosions of gun-powder. His confidence in Hugh was complete. Nor did he mind personal injuries. When on one occasion he was hurled against the sharp edge of a chair, cutting his head open badly, and his mother came to the rescue with indignation, sympathy and bandages, whilst accepting the latter he deprecated the two former, explaining apologetically, "It's only because my head's so big."

He admitted in after years to having felt most terribly swamped by the personalities of two of his brothers. The third he had more in common with, for he was more peace-loving, and he seemedto have more time to listen to the small boy's confidences and stories, which Donald started to write at the age of six.

Hugh, however, was his hero—a kind of demi-god. And truly there was something Greek about the boy—in his singular beauty of person, coupled with his brilliant mental equipment, and above all in the nothing less than Spartan methods with which, in spite of a highly sensitive temperament, he set himself to overcome his handicap of a naturally delicate physique and a bad head for heights. He turned himself out quite an athlete, and actually cured his bad head by a course of walking on giddy heights, preferably roofs—the parapet of the tall four-storied house the children lived in being a favourite training ground.

Donald was the apple of his eye, and he was quick to note a certain lack of vitality about the little boy—especially when he was growing fast—and a certain natural timidity. His letters from schoolare full of messages to and instructions concerning Donald's physical training, and from Sandhurst he would long to "run over and see after his boxing." He called him Don Diego, a name that suited the rather stately little fellow, and he used to fear sometimes that Donald was "getting too polite" and say he must "knock it out of him in the holidays." Needless to say, his handling of him was always very gentle.

The other over-vital brother, if a prime amuser, was also a prime tease, and being nearer Donald in age was also much less gentle.

Before very long these great personages took themselves off "zum neuen taten." But their Odysseys came home in the shape of letters, which, with their descriptions of strange countries and peoples and records of adventures—often the realization of boyish dreams—and also of difficulties overcome, were well calculated to appeal toDonald's childish imagination, and to increase his admiration for the writers—and also his feeling of impotence, and of the impossibility of being able to follow in the tracks of such giants among men!

His mother, however, was his never-failing confidante and friend. His love and admiration for her were unbounded, as for her courage, unselfishness and constant thought for others, more especially for the poor and insignificant among her neighbours. Though the humblest minded of women, she could, when occasion demanded, administer a rebuke with a decision and a fire that must have won the heartfelt admiration of her diffident little son.

He was not easily roused himself, but there is one instance of his being so that is eminently characteristic. He had come back from school evidently very perturbed, and at first his sister could get nothing out of him. But at last he flared up. His face reddened, his eyes burned like coalsand, in a voice trembling with rage, he said, "—— (naming a school-fellow) talks about things that I won't even think!"

At the age of about 14 he, too, went to Rugby, and there is an interesting prophecy about him by his brother Hugh belonging to this time. Hugh had by now earned a certain right to pronounce judgment, having already started to fulfil his early promise by making some mark as a soldier and a linguist. He had been invited to join the Egyptian Army at a critical time in the campaign of 1897-98, thanks to his proficiency in Arabic. His work was cut short by serious illness, the long period of convalescence after which he had utilized in working for and passing the Army Interpreter's examination in Turkish as well as the higher one in Arabic and his promotion exam. All of which achievements had been of use in helping him to wring out of the War Office a promise ofcertain distinguished service in China. In a letter home he writes:—

2ND BATT. THE ROYAL WARWICKSHIRE, REGT.,
THE CAMP,
COLCHESTER.
28th Sept., 1899.
MY DEAR MAMMA,—

I packed Donald off to school to-day in good time and cold-less.... He was wonderfully calm and collected. He was more at his ease in our mess than I should have been in a strange mess, and made himself agreeable to his neighbours without being forward. Also he looked very clean and smart, and was altogether quite a success.

That child has a future before him if his energy is up to form, which I hope. His philosophy is most amazing. He looks remarkably healthy, and is growing nicely....

Shortly after this letter was written the South African War broke out, and before six months were over the writer was killed in action, at the age of 27, whilstserving with the Mounted Infantry at Paardeberg.

It was the first sorrow of Donald's life, but six months later he was to suffer a yet more crushing blow in the loss of his dearly loved mother. The loss of his best confidante and his ideal seemed at first to stun the boy completely, and to cast him in upon himself entirely. Later on he remembered that he had felt at that time that he had nothing to say to any one. He had wondered what the others could have thought of him, and had thought how dreadfully unresponsive they must be finding him. His sister should have been of some use. But she can only think of herself then as of some strange figure, veiled and petrified with grief—grief not for her mother, but for the young hero whose magnetism had thrilled through every moment of her life—yet pointing onwards, with mutely insistent finger, to the path that her hero had trodden. And Donald, dazed alsohimself by grief—though from another cause—of his own accord, placed his first uncertain steps on the road that leads to military glory. No "voice" warned him as yet, and he had no other decisive leading.

If his sister failed him then, his father did not. Of him Donald wrote recently to an aunt, "Papa's letters to me are a heritage whose value can never diminish. His was indeed the pen of a ready writer, and in his case, as in the case of many rather reserved people, the pen did more justice to the man than the tongue. I never knew him until Mamma's death, when the weekly letter from him took the place of hers, and never stopped till I came home."

At Rugby, Donald was accounted a dreamer. Without the outlet he had hitherto had for his confidences and his thoughts no doubt the tendency to dream grew upon him. "Behold this dreamer cometh," was actually said of him by one of his masters.

Nevertheless there were happy timeswhen youth asserted itself and boyish friendships were made. In work he did well, for he entered the sixth form at the early age of 16-1/2, and was thereby enabled, though he left young, to have his name painted up "in hall" below those of his three brothers, and also on his "study" door which belonged to each of the four in turn.

He entered the Royal Military Academy, Woolwich, straight from Rugby, and before he was seventeen. We have his word for it that he was spiritually very unhappy there, finding evils with which he was impotent to grapple, going up as he did so young from school and before he had had time to acquire a "games" reputation—that all-important qualification for a boy if he wishes to influence his fellows. Nevertheless youthful spirits were bound to triumph sometimes. He was a perfectly sound and healthy, well-grown boy and a friend who was with him at "theShop" says he can remember no apparent trace of unhappiness, and is full of tales of his jokes and his fun, his quaint caricatures and doggerel rhymes, his love of flowers and nature, his hospitalities, and his joy in getting his friends to meet and know and like each other. Though he made no mark at Woolwich he did carry off the prize for the best essay on the South African War. With it he made his first appearance in print, for it was printed in the R.M.A. Magazine. While he was at Woolwich the family circle was enlarged by the arrival of a cousin from Australia, and she and Donald became the greatest of friends. She reminded him in some way of his mother, and this made all the difference.

The Island of Mauritius, to which he was sent at the age of twenty, not so very long after having received his commission in the Royal Garrison Artillery, stood for him later on, he has told us, as "Revelation"—"for there it was that I wasfirst a sceptic, and was first shown that I could not remain one." Also towards the end of his stay there, when he was doubting as to what course he should take, a sentence came to him insistently, "Would you know Christ? Lo, He is working in His vineyard." It was these things that decided him eventually to resign his commission, but of them his letters home make little or no mention. They are full, on the other hand, of descriptions of the beauties of the Island which, curious, odd, freakish and unexpected, held him as did those of no other place. The curious inconsistencies of the Creole nature also interested him, and he spent much of his spare time sketching and studying the people. Two friendships he made there were diverse and lasting, but he complains very much of feeling the lack of a woman friend—no one to tease and pick flowers for!

While he was still there, there appeared at home a baby nephew—another "Hugh"—"trailing clouds of glory," but to return all too soon to his "Eternal Home." Some years previously, when his eldest sister had told him of her engagement, he congratulated her warmly, and said he "had always longed for a nephew"! He never saw the child, but wrote after his death that he had heard so much about him that he seemed to know him, and "I think I must have played with him in my dreams." Possibly the baby nephew, in his short ten months of life, did more for his uncle than either knew, for no frozen hearts could do otherwise than melt in the presence of the insistent needs of that gallant little spirit and fragile little body, and a more whole-hearted sister was awaiting him on his return home, which took place at the end of two years, after he had fallen a victim to the prevalent complaint in the R.G.A—abscess on the liver. It was caused by the shocking conditions under which the R.G.A. had to live in Mauritius during that hot summer when the Russian Fleet sojourned in Madagascan waters, and in Donald's case it necessitated a severe operation.

His joy in his homecoming was quickly clouded over, for his father died only a month or two after his return; not, however, before he had given a delighted acquiescence to Donald's proposal to resign his commission and go to Oxford in order to study theology—his own favourite pursuit—with the object of eventually taking Holy Orders.

In the spring of 1907 Donald took a trip to Italy with his sister and a Rhodes Scholar cousin from Australia. It was the young men's first visit, and each brought back a special trophy: Donald's, a large photograph of a fine virile "Portrait of a man" by Giorgione in black and white, and his cousin, a sweet Madonna head by Luini.

Donald gave his sister her trophy on their return home, in remembrance of the lectures she had given the two of them on the pre-Raphaelite painters in Florence. It took the form of a water-colour caricature of herself, sitting enthroned in a Loggia as a sort of Sybil Saint with a halo and a book (Baedeker). Behind her, and outlined against a pale sky as seen through an archway of the Loggia in the typical Florentine fashion, are the blue mountains near Florence, some tall cypresses, a campanile and a castle perched on the top of a hill—all features of the landscapes through which they had passed together. In the foreground are himself and his cousin as monks adoring, also with haloes, and expressions of mock ecstasy!

On his return Donald went for a few months to Rugby House, the Rugby School Mission, in order to cram for Oxford. He thereby made a friend, and learned to love Browning.

After living so long at Brighton, and then in barracks, the beauty of Oxford was in itself alone a revelation to him. The work there, too, was entirely congenial. As a gunner subaltern he had been a square peg in a round hole. As regards the work there had been far too much to be accepted on authority for one of his fundamental type of mind; the relations existing between an officer and his men—in peace time, at any rate—seemed to him hardly human, and the making of quick decisions, which an officer is continually called upon to do, was then as always very difficult to him. His tastes, too, unusual in a subaltern, had made him rather lonely. He found much more in common with the undergraduate than with the subaltern. Going up as an "oldster" (22) was to him an advantage rather than otherwise, for his six years in the Army had given him a certain prestige which was a help to his natural diffidence, and helped to open more doors to him, so that he was not limited to any set.

He gained some reputation as a host, for he had the born host's gift of getting the right people together and making them feel at their ease. There was also, as a rule, some little individual touch about his entertainments that made them stand out. His manner, though naturally boyish and shy, could be both gay and debonair, quite irresistible in fact, when he was surrounded by congenial spirits! He played hockey, and was made a member of several clubs, sketched and made beautiful photographs. His time he divided strictly between the study of man and the study of theology, and though he did much hard, thorough and careful work in connexion with the latter, he always maintained that for a man who was going to be a parson the former was the more important study of the two.

He used, however, to complain much at this time of feeling himself incapable of any very strong emotion, even that of sorrow.

No doubt there is more stimulation to the brain than to the heart in the highly critical atmosphere of all phases of the intellectual life at Oxford; also Donald had hardly yet got over the shocks of his youth and the loneliness of his life abroad. He was, too, essentially and curiously the son of his father—even to his minor tastes, such as his connoisseur's palate for a good wine and his judgment in "smokes"—and this feeling of a certain detachment from the larger emotions of life was always his father's pose— the philosopher's. In his father's case it was perhaps engendered, if not necessitated, by his poor health and wretched nerves.

But can we not trace his dissatisfaction at this time in what he felt to be his cold philosophical attitude towards life to the same cause as much of the misery he suffered as a boy! In the paper he calls "School," which follows with that entitled "Home," he tells us how he would have liked to havechastised a school-fellow "had he dared," and his failure to dare was evidently what reduced him to the state of impotent rage described on page 9 of this sketch. Again at Woolwich, what made him unhappy was not so much the evils which he saw but his impotence to deal with them. So now again at Oxford he feels "impotent," impotent this time to feel and sympathize as he would have wished with suffering humanity. But within him was the light, "the light which is, of course, not physical," which betrayed itself through his wonderful smile—the same now as in babyhood; and from his mother, and perhaps also from the young country that gave her birth, he had inherited, as well as her great heart and broad human sympathies, the vigour that was to carry him through the experiences by means of which, in the fullness of time, that light, no longer dormant, was to break into a flame of infinite possibilities.

Donald's one complaint against Oxfordwas that the ideas that are born and generated there so often evaporate in talk and smoke. He left with the determination to "do," but before going on to a Clergy School he decided to accept a friend's invitation to visit him in savage Africa so that he might think things over, and put to the test, far away from the artificialities of Modern Life, the ideas he had assimilated in the highly sophisticated atmosphere of Oxford. As he quaintly put it: "Since Paul went into Arabia for three years, I don't see why I should not go to British East Africa for six months!" He did not, however, stay the whole time there, but re-visited his beloved Mauritius, and also stayed in Madagascar.

The beginning of 1911 found him at the Clergy School. But what he wanted he did not find there. During his Oxford vacations he had made many expeditions to poorer London, at first to Notting Dale where was the Rugby School Mission,and afterwards to Bermondsey. But these expeditions had not been entirely satisfactory. He had then gone as a "visitor." The lessons he wanted to learn now from "the People" could only be learned by becoming as far as possible one of them. The story of his struggles to do so in his life in Bermondsey, and of his journey to Australia in the steerage of a German liner and of his roughing it there, always with the same object in view, cannot be told here. The first outcome of it all was the writing of his book, The Lord of All Good Life. Of this book he says, in a letter to his friend Tom Allen of the Oxford and Bermondsey Mission:

"The book I regard as my child. I feel quite absurdly about it; to me it is the sudden vision of what lots of obscure things really meant. It is coming out of dark shadows into—moonlight ... I would have you to realize that it was written spontaneously in a burst, in sixweeks, without any consultation of authorities or any revision to speak of. I had tried and tried, but without success. Then suddenly everything cleared up. To myself, the writing of it was an illumination. I did not write it laboriously and with calculation or because I wanted to write a book and be an author. I wrote it because problems that had been troubling me suddenly cleared up and because writing down the result was to me the natural way of getting everything straight in my own mind."

The book was written not away in the peace of the country, nor in the comparative quiet of a certain sunny little sitting-room I know of, looking on to a leafy back garden in Kensington, where Donald often sat and

A STUDENT IN ARMS

smoked and wrote, but in a little flat in a dull tenement house in a grey street in Bermondsey, where I remember visiting him with a cousin of his.

Here the Student lived like a lord—for Bermondsey! For he possessed twoflats, one for his "butler"—a sick-looking young man in list slippers, and his wife and family—and the other for himself.

The little sitting-room in which he entertained us was very pleasant, with light walls, a bright table-cloth, a gleam of something brass that had come from Ceylon, one or two gaily painted dancing shields from Africa, and two barbaric looking dolls, about a foot high, dressed chiefly in beads and paint, that he had picked up in an Antananarivo shop in Madagascar. They came in usefully when he was lecturing on Missions!

His bedroom he did not want us to see. It struck cold and appeared to be reeking with damp!

The weather had been rather dull when we arrived, but suddenly there was a glint of sunshine, and a grind-organ that had wandered up the street started playing just opposite. Two couple of children began to dance. A girl with a jug stoppedto watch them, and mothers with babies came to their doors. A window was thrown open opposite and a whole family of children leaned out to see the fun.

Bermondsey was gay, and after we had gone the "Student" perpetuated the fact in a water-colour drawing which he sent to his cousin afterwards.

In the evening, however, the sounds would be more discordant, also the Student was running a Boys' Club, taking several Sunday services at the Mission, visiting some very sick people, and attending to a multifarious list of duties which left me breathless when I saw it, knowing too how many casual appeals always came to him and that he never was known to refuse a helping hand to any one! Nevertheless it was there, and in six weeks, that the Lord of All Good Life was written!

"Then came the war," and the Student shall tell us in his own words what it meant to him. Writing still to Tom Allen, whohad also enlisted, and afterwards also gave his life in the war, he says:

"For myself the war was, in a sense, a heaven-sent opportunity. Ever since I left Leeds I have been trying to follow out the theory that the proper subject of study for the theologian was man, and had increasingly been made to feel that nothing but violent measures could overcome my own shyness sufficiently to enable me to study outside my own class. Enlistment had always appealed to me as one of the few feasible methods of ensuring the desired results....

"I was interested to hear that you found the —— so illuminating as regards human potentialities for bestiality. I think that I plumbed the depths between sixteen and a half and twenty-two. I have learned nothing more since then about bestiality. In fact I am hardened, and, I am afraid, take it for granted. Since then I have been discovering humangoodness, which is

13

far more satisfactory. And oh, I have found it! In Bermondsey, in the stinking hold of the Zieten, in the wide, thirsty desert of Western Australia, and in the ranks of the 7th Battalion of the Rifle Brigade. I enlisted very largely to find out how far I really believed in the brotherhood of man when it comes to the point—and I do believe in it more and more."

Donald Hankey enlisted in August, 1914, and after a period of training, part of which was certainly the happiest time of his life, he went to the front in May, 1915, coming home wounded in August, when he wrote for the Spectator most of the articles that were published anonymously the following spring under the title of A Student in Arms. Before he left hospital he received a commission in his old regiment, the R.G.A., but still finding himself with no love for big guns, he transferred to his eldest brother's regiment, the Royal Warwickshire, hoping that by doing so he might get back to thefront the sooner. He did not, however, leave until May, 1916, after he had written his contribution to Faith or Fear.

Most of the numbers of the present volume were written in or near the trenches, and a fellow-officer gave his sister an interesting description of how it was done. "Your brother," said he, "will sit down in a corner of a trench, with his pipe, and write an article for the Spectator, or make funny sketches for his nephews and nieces, when none of the rest of us could concentrate sufficiently even to write a letter."

On October 6th, Donald Hankey wrote home: "We shall probably be fighting by the time you get this letter, but one has a far better chance of getting through now than in July. I shall be very glad if we do have a scrap, as we have been resting quite long enough. Of course one always has to face possibilities on such occasions; but we have faced them in advance, haven'twe? I believe with all my soul that whatever will be, will be for the best. As I said before, I should hate to slide meanly into winter without a scrap.... I have a top-hole platoon—nearly all young, and nearly all have been out here eighteen months—thoroughly good sporting fellows; so if I don't do well it will be my fault."

Six days after this the Student knelt down for a few seconds with his men— we have it on the testimony of one of them—and he told them a little of what was before them: "If wounded, 'Blighty'; if killed, the Resurrection." Then "over the top." He was last seen alive rallying his men, who had wavered for a moment under the heavy machine gun and rifle fire. He carried the waverers along with him, and was found that night close to the trench, the winning of which had cost him his life, with his platoon sergeant and a few of his men by his side.

What wonder that his cousin and best friend, when asked a short time previously what he was like, had replied, "He is the most beautiful thing that ever happened."

A STUDENT IN ARMS

AUTHOR'S FOREWORD

(Being Extracts from Letters to his Sister)

"I am very much wondering whether you will receive 'A Diary' in four parts. It is very much founded on fact, though altered in parts. You will probably be surprised at a certain change in tone, but remember that my previous articles were written in England, while this was written on the spot.... The Diary was not my diary, though it was so very nearly what mine might have been that it is difficult to say what is fiction and what is actuality in it. With regard to the 'conversation' during the bombardment, it represents in its totality what I believe the ordinary soldier feels. He loathes the war, and the grandiloquentspeeches of politicians irritate him by their failure to realize how loathesome war is. At the same time he knows he has got to go through with it, and only longs for the chance to hurry up. In the 'Diary,' again, I quite deliberately emphasized the depression of the man who thought he was being left out, and the mental effect of the clearing-up process because I thought that it would be a good thing for people to realize this side, and also partly because I felt that in previous articles I had glossed over it too much.... If I get a chance of publishing another book I shall certainly include them."

Note.—Not only "A Diary" and "Imaginary Conversations," but every paper in the present collection, with the exception of "The Wisdom," "The Potentate," and "A Passing in June," were written in France in 1916, and many of them actually in the trenches. The rough sketch for "A Passing in June" was written in France in 1915, but was completed when the author was in hospital at home.

"The Potentate" was written for the original volume of A Student in Arms, but was not published on account of its likeness in subject to Barrie's play, Der Tag, which, however, Donald had not seen or even heard of when he

DONALD HANKEY

wrote his own.

THE POTENTATE

The potentate1

SCENE. A tent (interior). The POTENTATE is sitting at a table listening to his COURT CHAPLAIN.

COURT CHAPLAIN (concluding his remarks). Where can we look for the Kingdom of God, Sire, if not among the German people? Consider your foes. The English are Pharisees, hypocrites. Woe to them, saith the Lord. The French are atheists. The Belgians are ignorant and priest-ridden. The Russians are sunk in mediæval superstition. As for the Italians, half are atheists and the other half idolators. Only in Germany do you find a reasonable and progressive faith,devoid of superstition, abreast of scientific thought, and of the highest ethical value. Germany then, Sire, is the Kingdom of God on earth. The Germans are the chosen people, the heirs of the promise, and let their enemies be scattered!

(The POTENTATE rises, leans forward with his hands on the table, and an expression of extreme gratification, while the CHAPLAIN stands with a smug and respectful smile on his white face.)

POTENTATE. You are right, my dear Clericus, abundantly right. Very well put indeed! Yes, Germany is the Kingdom of God, and I (drawing himself up to his full height)—I am Germany! The strength of the Lord is in my right arm, and He teaches it terrible things for the unbeliever and the hypocrite. With God I conquer! Good-night, my dear Clericus, good-night.

(CLERICUS departs with a low bow, and the POTENTATE sinks into his chair with a gesture of fatigue. Enter a GENERAL of the Headquarters Staff with telegrams.)

POTENTATE (brightening). Ha, my dear General, you have news?

GENERAL. Excellent news, Sire! On the Eastern front the Russians continue to give way. In the West a French attack has been repulsed with heavy loss, and our gallant Prussians have driven the British out of half a mile of trenches.

(At this last bit of news the POTENTATE springs to his feet with a look of joy.)

POTENTATE. A sign! My God, a sign! Pardon, General, I was thinking of a conversation that I have just had with Dr. Clericus. Come now, show me where these trenches are.

(The GENERAL produces a map, over which they pore together.)

POTENTATE. Excellent, excellent! A most valuable capture. Our losses were ...?

GENERAL. Slight, Sire.

POTENTATE. Better and better. I cannot afford to lose my good Prussians, my heroic, my invincible Prussians. To what do you attribute the success?

GENERAL. The success was due in a large measure to the perfection of the apparatus suggested a week ago by your Majesty's scientific adviser.

POTENTATE (blanching a little). Ah, then it was not a charge, eh?

GENERAL. The charge followed, Sire; but the work was already done. The defenders of the trench were already dead or dying before our heroes reached it.

POTENTATE (sinking back in his chair with his finger to his lips, and a slight frown). Thank you, General, your news is of the best. I will detain you no longer. (TheGENERAL bows.) Stay! Has a counterattack been launched yet?

GENERAL. Not yet, Sire. No doubt one will be attempted to-night. Our men are prepared.

POTENTATE. Good. Bring me fresh news as soon as it arrives. Good-night, General, good-night.

(Exit GENERAL.)

(The POTENTATE sits musing for a considerable time. A slight cough is heard, and he raises his head.)

POTENTATE (slowly). Enter!

(Enter a tall figure in a long black academic gown and black clothes.)

POTENTATE (with an attempt at gaiety). Come in, my dear Sage, come in. You are welcome. (A little anxiously) You have the crystal? Good. How is theMaster? Still busy devising new means of victory?

THE SAGE. My master's poor skill is always at your service, Sire. You have only to command.

POTENTATE. I know it. Now let me have the crystal. I would see if possible the scene of to-day's victory in Flanders.

(The SAGE hands him the crystal with a low bow. The POTENTATE seizes it eagerly, and gazes into it. A pause.)

POTENTATE (raising his head suddenly). Horrible, horrible!

SAGE. Sire?

POTENTATE. This last invention of your master's is inhuman!

SAGE. War is inhuman, Sire. Where a speedy end is desired, is it not kindest to be cruel?

(The POTENTATE gazes again into the crystal,but starts up immediately with a gasp of horror.)

POTENTATE. Again the same vision! Always after my victories the vision of the Crucified, with the stern reproachful eyes! Am I not the Lord's appointed instrument? What means it? Tell your master that I will have no more of his inventions. They are too diabolical! They imperil my cause!

SAGE (pointing to the crystal). Look again, Sire.

POTENTATE (gazing into the crystal, and in a low and agonized voice). Time with his scythe raised menacingly against me. (Abruptly) This is a trickery, Sirrah! Have a care! But I will not be tricked. Are my troops not brave? Are they not invincible? Can they not win by their proven valour? Who can stand against them, for the strength of the Lord is in their right hands?

(Enter GENERAL hastily)

GENERAL. Sire.... (He starts, and stops short).

POTENTATE (testily). Go on, go on. What is it?

GENERAL. Sire, the English counterattack has for the moment succeeded. Infuriated by their defeat they fought so that no man could resist them. They have regained the trenches they had lost, but we hope to attack again to-morrow, when—

POTENTATE. Enough! Leave me!

(The GENERAL withdraws, and the POTENTATE leans forward with his head on his hands.)

SAGE (commiseratingly). Apparently other troops are brave besides your own, Sire!

POTENTATE (brokenly). The cowards!The cowards! Five nations against three! Alas, my poor Prussians!

SAGE. If you will look once more into the crystal, Sire, I think you will see something that will interest you.

(The POTENTATE takes the crystal again, but without confidence.)

POTENTATE (in a slow recitative). A stricken field by night. The dead lie everywhere, German and English, side by side. But all are not dead. Some are but wounded. They help one another. Prussian and Briton help one another, with painful smiles on their white faces. What? Have they forgotten their hate? My Prussians! Can you so soon forget? I mourn for you! But who are these? White figures, vague, elusive! See, they seem to come down from above. They are carrying away the souls of my Prussians! And of the accursed English!What! One Paradise for both! Impossible! And

who is that watching? He who with a smile so loving, and yet so stern ...
Ah!... My God ... no!... not I....

(The POTENTATE rises with a strangled cry, and sinks into his chair a nerveless wreck. The SAGE watches coolly, with a cynical smile.)

SAGE. So, Sire, you must find room for the English in that kingdom of yours and God's! Perchance it is more catholic than we had thought!

(The POTENTATE groans.)

SAGE. Sire, you have seen some truth to-night. Is courage, is God, all on your side? Is Time on your side? Shall I go back to my master and tell him that you need no more of his inventions?

(He pauses, and glances at the POTENTATE with a look of contempt, and then turns to go. The POTENTATE looks round him with a ghastly stare.)

POTENTATE (feebly). No ... the Crucified ... Time ... Stay, stay!

(The SAGE turns with a gesture of triumph.)

(Curtain.)

Footnote 1:

It is necessary to state that The Potentate was written before Sir James Barrie's play Der Tag appeared.

THE BAD SIDE OF MILITARY SERVICE

A Padre who has earned the right to talk about the "average Tommy," writes to me that A Student in Arms gives a very one-sided picture of him. While cordially admitting his unselfishness, his good comradeship, his patience, and his pluck, my friend challenges me to deny that military, and especially active, service often has a brutalizing effect on the soldier, weakening his moral fibres, and causing him to sink to a low animal level.

Those who are in the habit of reading between the lines will, I think, often have seen the shadow of this darker side of army life on the pages of A Student in Arms; but I have not written of it specificallyfor several reasons. It will suffice if I mention two. First, I was writing mainly of the private and the N.C.O. Rightly or wrongly, I imagined that those for whom I was writing were in the habit of taking for granted this darker side of life in the ranks. I imagined that they thought of the "lower classes" as being naturally coarser and more animal than the "upper classes." I wanted then, and I want now, to contradict that belief with all the vehemence of which I am capable. Officers and men necessarily develop different qualities, different forms of expression, different mental attitudes. But I am confident that I speak the truth when I say that essentially, and in the eyes of God there is nothing to choose between them.

If I must write of the brutalizing effect of war on the soldier, let it be clearly understood that I am speaking, not of officers only, nor of privates only, but offighting men of every class and rank. As a matter of fact I have never, whether before or during the war, belonged to a mess where the tone was cleaner or more wholesome than it was in the Sergeants' Mess of my old battalion.

My second reason for not writing about the bad side of Army life was that mere condemnation is so futile. I have listened to countless sermons in which the "lusts of the flesh" were denounced, and have known for certain that their power for good was nil. If I write about it now, it is only because I hope that I may be able to make clearer the causes and processes of such moral deterioration as exists, and thus to help those who are trying to combat it, to do so with greater understanding and sympathy.

Even in England most officers, and all privates, are cut off from their womenfolk. Mothers, sisters, wives, and sweethearts are inaccessible. All have a certain amount of leisure, and very little to do with it.All are physically fit and mentally rather unoccupied. All are living under an unnatural discipline from which, when the last parade of the day is over, there is a natural reaction. Finally, wherever there are troops, and especially in war time, there are "bad" women and weak women. The result is inevitable. A certain number of both officers and men "go wrong."

Fifteen months ago I was a private quartered in a camp near Aldershot. After tea it began to get dark. The tent was damp, gloomy, and cold. The Y.M.C.A. tent and the Canteen tent were crowded. One wandered off to the town. The various soldiers' clubs were filled and overflowing. The bars required more cash than one possessed. The result was that one spent a large part of one's evenings wandering aimlessly about the streets. Fortunately I discovered an upper room in a Wesleyan soldiers' home, where there was generally quiet, and an empty chair.I shall always be grateful to that "home," for the many hours which I whiled away there with a book and a pipe. But most of us spent a great deal of our leisure, bored and impecunious, "on the streets"; and if a fellow ran up against "a bit of skirt," he was generally just in the mood to follow it wherever it might lead. The moral of this is, double your subscriptions to the Y.M.C.A., Church huts, soldiers' clubs, or whatever organization you fancy! You will be helping to combat vice in the only sensible way.

I don't suppose that the officers were much better off than we were. Their tents may have been a little lighter and less crowded than ours. They had a late dinner to occupy part of the long evening. They had more money to spend, and perhaps more to occupy their minds. But I fancy that as great a proportion of them as of us took the false step; and though perhaps when they compared notes theirlanguage may have been less blunt than ours, I am not sure that, for this very reason, it may not have been more poisonous. But mind you, we did not all go wrong, by any means, though I believe that some fellows did, both officers and men, who would not have done so if they had stayed at home with their mothers, sisters, sweethearts, or wives.

So much for the Army at home. When we cross the Channel every feature is a hundred times intensified. Consider the fighting man in the trenches— and I am still speaking of both officers and men—the most ordinary refinements of life are conspicuously absent. There is no water to wash in.

Vermin abound, sleeping and eating accommodations are frankly disgusting. One is obliged for the time to live like a pig. Added to this one is all the time in a state of nervous tension. One gets very little sleep. Every night has its anxieties and responsibilities. Dangeror death may come at any moment. So for a week or a fortnight or a month, as the case may be. Then comes the return to billets, to comparative safety and comfort—the latter nothing to boast about though! Tension is relaxed. There is an inevitable reaction. Officers and men alike determine to "gather rosebuds" while they may. Their bodies are fit, their wills are relaxed. If they are built that way, and an opportunity offers, they will "satisfy the lusts of the flesh."

When there is real fighting to be done the dangers of the after-reaction are intensified. You who sit at home and read of glorious bayonet charges do not realize what it means to the man behind the bayonet. You don't realize the repugnance for the first thrust—a repugnance which has got to be overcome. You don't realize the change that comes over a man when his bayonet is wet with the blood of his first enemy. He "sees red." The primitive"blood-lust," kept under all his life by the laws and principles of peaceful society, surges through his being, transforming him, maddening him with the desire to kill, kill, kill! Ask any one who has been through it if this is not true. And that letting loose of a primitive lust is not going to be without its effect on a man's character.

At the same time, of course, not all of us become animals out here. There are other influences at work. Caring for the wounded, burying the mutilated dead, cause one to hate war, and to value ten times more the ways of peace. Many are saved from sinking in the scale, by a love of home which is able to bridge the gulf which separates them from their beloved. The letters of my platoon are largely love letters—often the love letters of married men to their wives.

There is immorality in the Army; when there is opportunity immorality is rife. Possibly there is more abroad than there isat home. If so it is because there is far greater temptation. Nevertheless, I fancy that my correspondent, who is a padre, a don, and at least the beginning of a saint, is perhaps inclined to exaggerate the extent of the evil in the Army as compared with civil life. I imagine that very few padres, especially if they are dons, and most of all if they are saints, realize that in civil life as in Army life, the average man is immoral, both in thought and deed. Let us be frank about this. What a doctor might call the "appetites" and a padre the "lusts" of the body, hold dominion over the average man, whether civilian or soldier, unless they are counteracted by a stronger power. The only men who are pure are those who are absorbed in some pursuit, or possessed by a great love; be it the love of clean, wholesome life which is religion, or the love of a noble man which is hero-worship, or the love of a true woman. These are the four powerswhich are stronger than "the flesh"—the zest of a quest, religion, hero-worship, and the love of a good woman. If a man is not possessed by one of these he will be immoral.

Probably most men are immoral. The conditions of military, and especially of active service merely intensify the temptation. Unless a soldier is wholly devoted to the cause, or powerfully affected by religion, or by hero-worship, or by pure love, he is immoral.

Perhaps most men are immoral if they get the chance. Most soldiers are immoral if they get the chance. But those who are trying to help the soldier can do so with a good heart if they realize that in him they have a foundation on which to build. Already he is half a hero-worshipper. Already he half believes in the beauty of sacrifice and in the life immortal. Already he is predisposed to value exceedingly all that savours of clean, wholesomehome life. On that foundation it should be possible to build a strong idealism which shall prevail against the flesh. And this is my last word—it is by building up, and not by casting down, that the soldier can be saved from degradation. The devil that possesses so many can only be cast out by an angel that is stronger than he.

THE GOOD SIDE OF MILITARISM

I had a letter the other day from an Oxford friend. In it was this phrase: "I loathe militarism in all its forms." Somehow it took me back quite suddenly to the days before the war, to ideas that I had almost completely forgotten. I suppose that in those days the great feature of those of us who tried to be "in the forefront of modern thought" was their riotous egotism, their anarchical insistence on the claims of the individual at the expense even of law, order, society, and convention. "Self-realization" we considered to be the primary duty of every man and woman.

The wife who left her husband, children,and home because of her passion for another man was a heroine, braving the hypocritical judgments of society to assert the claims of the individual soul. The woman who refused to abandon all for love's sake, was not only a coward but a criminal, guilty of the deadly sin of sacrificing her soul, committing it to a prison where it would languish and never blossom to its full perfection. The man who was bound to uncongenial drudgery by the chains of an early marriage or aged parents dependent on him, was the victim of a tragedy which drew tears from our eyes. The woman who neglected her home because she needed a "wider sphere" in which to develop her personality was a champion of women's rights, a pioneer of enlightenment. And, on the other hand, the people who went on making the best of uncongenial drudgery, or in any way subjected their individualities to what old-fashioned people calledduty, were in our eyes contemptible poltroons.

It was the same in politics and religion. To be loyal to a party or obedient to a Church was to stand self-confessed a fool or a hypocrite. Self-realization, that was in our eyes the whole duty of man.

And then I thought of what I had seen only a few days before. First, of battalions of men marching in the darkness, steadily and in step, towards the roar of the guns; destined in the next twelve hours to charge as one man, without hesitation or doubt, through barrages of cruel shell and storms of murderous bullets. Then, the following afternoon, of a handful of men, all that was left of about three battalions after ten hours of fighting, a handful of men exhausted, parched, strained, holding on with grim determination to the last bit of German trench, until they should receive the order toretire. And lastly, on the days and nights following, of the constant streams of wounded and dead being carried down the trench; of the unceasing search that for three or four days was never fruitless.

Self-realization! How far we have travelled from the ideals of those pre-war days. And as I thought things over I wondered at how faint a response that phrase, "I loathe militarism in all its forms," found in my own mind.

Before the war I too hated "militarism." I despised soldiers as men who had sold their birthright for a mess of pottage. The sight of the Guards drilling in Wellington Barracks, moving as one man to the command of their drill instructor, stirred me to bitter mirth. They were not men but manikins. When I first enlisted, and for many months afterwards, the "mummeries of military discipline," the saluting, the meticulous uniformity, the rigid suppression of individualexuberance, chafed and infuriated me. I compared it to a ritualistic religion, a religion of authority only, which depended not on individual assent but on tradition for its sanctions. I loathed militarism in all its forms. Now ... well, I am inclined to reconsider my judgment. Seeing the end of military discipline, has shown me something of its ethical meaning—more than that, of its spiritual meaning.

For though the part of the "great push" that it fell to my lot to see was not a successful part, it was none the less a triumph—a spiritual triumph. From the accounts of the ordinary war correspondent I think one hardly realizes how great a spiritual triumph it was. For the war correspondent only sees the outside, and can only describe the outside of things. We who are in the Army, who know the men as individuals, who have talked with them, joked with them,censored their letters, worked with them, lived with them we see below the surface.

The war correspondent sees the faces of the men as they march towards the Valley of the Shadow, sees the steadiness of eye and mouth, hears the cheery jest. He sees them advance into the Valley without flinching. He sees some of them return, tired, dirty, strained, but still with a quip for the passer-by. He gives us a picture of men without nerves, without sensitiveness, without imagination, schooled to face death as they would face rain or any trivial incident of everyday life. The "Tommy" of the war correspondent is not a human being, but a lay figure with a gift for repartee, little more than the manikin that we thought him in those far-off days before the war, when we watched him drilling on the barrack square. We soldiers know better. We know that each one of those men is an individual, full of human affections, manyof them writing tender letters home every week, each one longing with all his soul for the end of this hateful business of war which divides him from all that he loves best in life. We know that every one of these men has a healthy individual's repugnance to being maimed, and a human shrinking from hurt and from the Valley of the Shadow of Death.

The knowledge of all this does not do away with the even tread of the troops as they pass, the steady eye and mouth, the cheery jest; but it makes these a hundred times more significant. For we know that what these things signify is not lack of human affection, or weakness, or want of imagination, but something superimposed on these, to which they are wholly subordinated. Over and above the individuality of each man, his personal desires and fears and hopes, there is the corporate personality of the soldier which knows no fear and only oneambition—to defeat the enemy, and so to further the righteous cause for which he is fighting. In each of those men there is this dual personality: the ordinary human ego that hates danger and shrinks from hurt and death, that longs for home, and would welcome the end of the war on any terms; and also the stronger personality of the soldier who can tolerate but one end to this war, cost what that may—the victory of liberty and justice, and the utter abasement of brute force.

And when one looks back over the months of training that the soldier has had, one recognizes how every feature of it, though at the time it often seemed trivial and senseless and irritating, was in reality directed to this end. For from the moment that a man becomes a soldier his dual personality begins. Henceforth he is both a man and a soldier. Before his training is complete the order mustbe reversed, and he must be a soldier and a man. As a soldier he must obey and salute those whom, as a man, he very likely dislikes and despises. In his conduct he no longer only has to consider his reputation as a man, but still more his honour as a soldier. In all the conditions of his life, his dress, appearance, food, drink, accommodation, and work, his individual preferences count for nothing, his efficiency as a soldier counts for everything. At first he "hates" this, and "can't see the point of" that. But by the time his training is complete he has realized that whether he hates a thing or not, sees the point of a thing or not, is a matter of the uttermost unimportance. If he is wise, he keeps his likes and dislikes to himself.

All through his training he is learning the unimportance of his individuality, realizing that in a national, a world crisis, it counts for nothing. On the otherhand, he is equally learning that as a unit in a fighting force his every action is of the utmost importance. The humility which the Army inculcates is not an abject self-depreciation that leads to loss of self-respect and effort. Substituted for the old individualism is a new self-consciousness. The man has become humble, but in proportion the soldier has become exceeding proud. The old personal whims and ambitions give place to a corporate ambition and purpose, and this unity of will is symbolized in action by the simultaneous exactitude of drill, and in dress by the rigid identity of uniform. Anything which calls attention to the individual, whether in drill or in dress, is a crime, because it is essential that the soldier's individuality should be wholly subordinated to the corporate personality of the regiment. As I said before, the personal humility of the soldier has nothing in it of abject self-depreciation or slackness. On thecontrary, every detail of his appearance, and every most trivial feature of his duty assumes an immense significance. Slackness in his dress and negligence in his work are military crimes. In a good regiment the soldier is striving after perfection all the time.

And it is when he comes to the supreme test of battle that the fruits of his training appear. The good soldier has learnt the hardest lesson of all—the lesson of self-subordination to a higher and bigger personality. He has learnt to sacrifice everything which belongs to him individually to a cause that is far greater than any personal ambitions of his own can ever be. He has learnt to do this so thoroughly that he knows no fear—for fear is personal. He has learnt to "hate" father and mother and life itself for the sake of—though he may not call it that—the Kingdom of God on earth.

It is a far cry from the old days whenone talked of self-realization, isn't it? I make no claim to be a good soldier; but I think that perhaps I may be beginning to be one; for if I am asked now whether I "loathe militarism in all its forms," I think that "the answer is in the negative," I will even go farther, and say that I hope that some of the discipline and self-subordination that have availed to send men calmly to their death in war, will survive in the days of peace, and make of those who are left better citizens, better workmen, better servants of the State, better Church men.

A MONTH'S REFLECTIONS

Timothy and I are on detachment. We are billeted with M. le Curé, and we mess at the schoolmaster's. Hence we are on good terms with all parties, for of course a good schoolmaster shrugs his shoulders at a priest, and a good priest returns the compliment. In war time, however, the hatchet seems to be buried pretty deep. We have not seen it sticking out anywhere.

M. le Curé has a beautiful rose garden, a cask of excellent cider, a passable Sauterne, and a charming pony. He is a good fellow, I should think, though without much education. His house—or what I have seen of it—is the exact opposite of what an English country vicar's would be. The only sitting-room that I have seen is as neat as an old maid's. There is a polished floor, an oval polished table on which repose four large albums at regular intervals, each on its own little mat. There is a mantelpiece with gilt candlesticks and an ornate clock under a glass dome. Round the walls are photographs of brother clergy, the place of honour being assigned to a stout Chanoine. The chairs are stiff and uncomfortable. One of them, which is more imposing and uncomfortable than the rest, is obviously for the Bishop when he comes. There are no papers, no books, no ash-trays, no confusion. I have never seen M. le Curé sit there. I fancy he lives in the kitchen and in his garden.

Timothy sleeps in the bed which the Bishop uses, and is told he ought to feel très saint.

The wife of the schoolmaster cooks for us. She is an excellent soul. We give her full marks. She has a smile and an omelette for every emergency, and waves aside all Timothy's vagaries with "Ah, monsieur, la jeunesse!" I am not sure that Timothy quite likes it!

Timothy is immense. He is that rarest of birds, a wholly delightful egotist. He is the sun, but we all bask and shine with reflected glory. The men are splendid, because they are his men. I am a great success because I am his subaltern. Fortunately we all have a sense of humour and so are highly pleased with ourselves and each other. After all, if one is a Captain at twenty-two ...! But he's a good soldier, too, and we all believe in him. Timothy's all right, in spite of la jeunesse!

Rain! The men are fifteen in a tent in a sea of mud. Poor beggars! They are having a thin time. Working parties in the trenches day and night; every one soaked to the skin; and then a returnto a damp, crowded, muddy tent. No pay, no smokes, and yet they are wonderfully cheery, and all think that the "Push" is going to end the war. I wish I thought so!

These rats are the limit! The dugout swarms with them. Last night they ate half my biscuits and a good part of Timothy's clean socks, and whenever I began to get to sleep one of them would run across my face, or some other sensitive part of my anatomy, and wake me up. I shall leave the candle alight to-night, to see if that keeps them away.

Last night the rats tried to eat the candle, and very nearly set me on fire. If it were not for the rain I would try the firestep.

The men are having a rotten time again—no proper shelter from the rain, and short rations, to say nothing of remarkably good practice by the Boche artillery. C——,just out from England, got scuppered this afternoon. A good boy—made his communion just before we came in. I suppose he didn't know much about it, and that he is really better off now; but at the same time it makes one angry.

The rain has lifted, so last night I tried the firestep, and got a good sleep. The absurd thing was that I couldn't wake up properly. I came on duty at midnight, was roused, got to my feet, and started to walk along the trench. And then the Nameless Terror, that lurks in dark corners when one is a small boy, gripped me. I was frightened of the dark, filled with a sense of impending disaster! It took about ten minutes to wake properly and shake it off. I must try to get more sleep somehow; but it is jolly difficult.

The great bombardment has begun, the long-promised strafing of the Boche. Accordingto the gunners they will all be dead, buried, or dazed when the time comes for us to go over the top. I doubt it! If they have enough deep dug-outs I don't fancy that the bombardment will worry them very much.

Now we are at rest for a day or two before the Push. I am to be left out—in charge of carriers. Damn! I might as well be A.S.C. I see myself counting ration bags while the battalion is charging with fixed bayonets; and in the evening sending up parties of weary laden carriers over shell-swept areas, while I myself stay behind at the Dump. Damn! Damn!! Damn!!! Then I shall receive ironical congratulations on my "cushy" job.

Have just seen the battalion off. I don't start for another five hours. I loathe war. It is futile, idiotic. I would gladly be out of the Army to-morrow. Glory is apainted idol, honour a phantasy, religion a delusion. We wallow in blood and torture to please a creature of our imagination. We are no better than South Sea Islanders.

Just here the attack was a failure. When I got to the Dump I found the battalion still there. By an irony of fate I was the only officer of my company to set foot in the German lines. After a day of idleness and depression I had to detail a party to carry bombs at top speed to some relics of the leading battalions, who were still clinging to the extremest corner of the enemy's front line some distance to our left. Being fed up with inaction, I took the party myself. It was a long way. The trenches were choked with wounded and stragglers and troops who had never been ordered to advance. In many places they were broken down by shell-fire, in others they were waist-deep in water. By dint of much shouting and shoving and cursing I managedto get through with about ten of my men, but had to leave the others to follow with a sergeant.

At last we sighted our objective, a cluster of chalk mounds surrounded with broken wire, shell craters, corpses, wreathed in smoke, dotted with men. I think we all ran across the ground between our front line and our objective, though it must have been more or less dead ground. Anyhow, only one man was hit. When we got close the scene was absurdly like a conventional battle picture—the sort of picture that one never believes in for a minute. There was a wild mixture of regiments—Jocks, Irishmen, Territorials, etc., etc. There was no proper trench left. There were rifles, a machine gun, a Lewis rifle, and bombs all going at the same time. There were wounded men sitting in a kind of helpless stupor; there were wounded trying to drag themselves back to our own lines; there were the dead of whom no one took any notice. But the prevailingnote was one of utter weariness coupled with dogged tenacity.

Here and there were men who were self-conscious, wondering what would become of themselves. I was one of them, and we were none the better for it. Most of the fellows, though, had forgotten themselves. They no longer flinched, or feared. They had got beyond that. They were just set on clinging to that mound and keeping the Huns at bay until their officer gave the word to retire. Their spirit was the spirit of the oarsman, the runner, or the footballer, who has strained himself to the utmost, who if he stopped to wonder whether he could go on or not would collapse; but who, because he does not stop to wonder, goes on miraculously long after he should, by all the laws of nature, have succumbed to sheer exhaustion.

Having delivered my bombs into eager hands, I reported to the officer who seemed to be in charge, and asked if I could doanything. I must frankly admit that my one hope was that he would not want me to stay. He began to say how that morning he had reached his objective, and how for lack of support on his flank, for lack of bombs, for lack of men, he had been forced back; and how for eight hours he had disputed every inch of ground till now his men could only cling to these mounds with the dumb mechanical tenacity of utter exhaustion. "You might go to H.Q.," he said at last, "and tell them where I am, and that I can't hold on without ammunition and a barrage."

I am afraid that I went with joy on that errand. I did not want to stay on those chalk mounds.

I only saw a very little bit of the battle. Thank God it has gone well elsewhere; but here we are where we started. Day and night we have done nothing but bring in the wounded and the dead. When one seesthe dead, their limbs crushed and mangled, their features distorted and blackened, one can only have repulsion for war. It is easy to talk of glory and heroism when one is away from it, when memory has softened the gruesome details. But here, in the presence of the mutilated and tortured dead, one can only feel the horror and wickedness of war. Indeed it is an evil harvest, sown of pride and arrogance and lust of power. Maybe through all this evil and pain we shall be purged of many sins. God grant it! If ever there were martyrs, some of these were martyrs, facing death and torture as ghastly as any that confronted the saints of old, and facing it with but little of that fierce fanatical exaltation of faith that the early Christians had to help them.

For these were mostly quiet souls, loving their wives and children and the little comforts of home life most of all, little stirred by great emotions or passions. Yet they hadsome love for liberty, some faith in God,—not a high and flaming passion, but a quiet insistent conviction. It was enough to send them out to face martyrdom, though their lack of imagination left them mercifully ignorant of the extremity of its terrors. It was enough, when they saw their danger in its true perspective, to keep them steadfast and tenacious.

For them "it is finished." R.I.P.

ROMANCE

I suppose that there are very few officers or men who have been at the front for any length of time who would not be secretly, if not openly, relieved and delighted if they "got a cushy one" and found themselves en route for "Blighty"; yet in many ways soldiering at the front is infinitely preferable to soldiering at home. One of the factors which count most heavily in favour of the front, is the extraordinary affection of officers for their men.

In England, officers hardly know their men. They live apart, only meet on parade, and their intercourse is carried on through the prescribed channels. Even if you do get keen on a particular squad ofrecruits, or a particular class of would-be bombers, you lose them so soon that your enthusiasm never ripens into anything like intimacy. But at the front you have your own platoon; and week after week, month after month, you are living in the closest proximity; you see them all day, you get to know the character of each individual man and boy, and the result in nearly every case is this extraordinary affection of which I have spoken.

You will find it in the most unlikely subjects. I have heard a Major, a Regular with, as I thought, a good deal of regimental stiffness, talk about his men with a voice almost choked with emotion. "When you see what they have to put up with, and how amazingly cheery they are through it all, you feel that you can't do enough for them. They make you feel that you're not fit to black their boots." And then he went on to tell how it was often the fellows whom in England you had despaired of, fellows whowere always "up at orders," who out at the front became your right-hand men, the men on whom you found yourself relying.

I had a letter not long ago from a gunner Captain, also a Regular, who has been out almost since the beginning of the war. He wrote: "One of my best friends has just been killed"; and the "best friend" was not the fellow he had known at "the shop," or played polo with in India, or hunted with in Ireland, but a scamp of a telephonist, who had stolen his whisky and owned up; who had risked his life for him, who had been a fellow-sportsman who could be relied on in a tight corner in the most risky of all games.

There is indeed a glamour and a pathos about the private soldier, especially when, as so often happens, he is really only a boy. When you meet him in the trenches, wet, covered with mud, with tired eyes speaking of long watches and hours of risky work, he never fails to greet youwith a smile, and you love him for it, and feel that nothing you can do can make up to him for it. For you have slept in a much more comfortable place than he has. You have had unlimited tobacco and cigarettes. You have had a servant to cook for you. You have fared sumptuously compared with him. You don't feel his superior. You don't want to be "gracious without undue familiarity." Exactly what you want to do is a bit doubtful—the Major said he wanted to black his boots for him, and that is perhaps the best way of expressing it.

When he goes over the top and works away in front of the parapet with the moon shining full and the machine guns busy all along; when he gets back to billets, and throws off his cares and bathes and plays games like any irresponsible schoolboy; even when he breaks bounds and is found by the M.P. skylarking in ——, you can't help loving him. Most of all,when he lies still and white with a red stream trickling from where the sniper's bullet has made a hole through his head, there comes a lump in your throat that you can't swallow; and you turn away so that you shan't have to wipe the tears from your eyes.

Gallant souls, those boys, and all the more gallant because they hate war so much. Their nerves quiver when a shell or a "Minnie" falls into the trench near them, and then they smile to hide their weakness. They hate going over the parapet when the machine guns are playing; so they don't hesitate, but plunge over with a smile to hide their fears. Their cure for every mental worry is a smile, their answer to every prompting of fear is a plunge. They have no philosophy or fanaticism to help them—only the sporting instinct which is in every healthy British boy.

Then there are "the old men," less attractive, less stirring to the imagination,less sensitive, but who grow upon you more and more as you get to know them. Any one over twenty-three or so is an "old man." They have lost the grace, the irresponsibility, the sensibility of youth. Their eyes and mouths are steadier, their movements more deliberate. But they are the fellows whom you would choose for a patrol, or a raid, where a cool head and a stout heart are what is wanted. It takes you longer to know these. They are less responsive to your advances. But when you have tested them and they have tested you, you know that you have that which is stronger

A STUDENT IN ARMS

than any terror of night or day, a loyalty which nothing can shake.

And then when he thinks how little he deserves all this love and loyalty, the subaltern's heart aches with a feeling that can find no expression either in word or deed.

This is a tale that has often been told, and that people in England know byheart. It cannot be told too often. It cannot be learnt too well. For the time will come when we shall need to remember it, and when it will be easy to forget. Will you remember it, O ye people, when the boy has become a man, and the soldier has become a workman? But there are other tales to tell. There are the tales of the sergeant-major and the sergeants, the corporals and the "lance-jacks." Sergeant-majors, sergeants, and corporals are not romantic figures. If you think of them at all, you probably think of rumjars and profanity. Yet they are the very backbone of the Army. I have been a sergeant and I have been a private soldier, and I know that the latter has much the better time of the two. He at least has the kind of liberty which belongs to utter irresponsibility. If he breaks bounds in the exuberance of his spirits, no one thinks much worse of him as long as he does not make a song about paying the penalty!

Of course he has to be punished. So many days of sleeping in the guard tent, extra fatigues, pack-drill, and perhaps a couple of hours tied up, as an example to evil-doers. But if he has counted the cost, and pays the price with a grin, we just say "Young scamp!" and dismiss the matter. But if a sergeant or a corporal does the same, that's a very different matter. He has shown himself unfit for his job. He has betrayed a trust. We cannot forgive him. Responsibility has its disadvantages. The senior N.C.O. gets no relaxation from discipline. In the line and out of it he must always be watchful, self-controlled, orderly. He must never wink. These men have not the glamour of the boy private; but their high sense of duty and discipline, their keenness and efficiency, merit all the honour that we can give them.

Finally—for it would not do for a subaltern to discuss his superiors—we cometo the junior officer. Somehow I fancy that in the public eye he too is a less romantic figure than the private. One does not associate him with privations and hardships, but with parcels from home. Well, it is quite right. He has such a much less uncomfortable time than his men that he does not deserve or want sympathy on that score. He is better off in every way. He has better quarters, better food, more kit, a servant, and in billets far greater liberty. And yet there is many a man who is now an officer who looks back on his days as a private with regret. Could he have his time over again ... yes, he would take a commission; but he would do so, not with any thought for the less hardship of it, but from a stern sense of duty—the sense of duty which does not allow a man with any self-respect to refuse to shoulder a heavier burden when called upon to do so.

Those apparently irresponsible subalternswhom you see entertaining their lady friends at the Canton or Ciro's do, when they are at the front, have very heavy responsibilities. Even in the ordinary routine of trench life, so many decisions have to be made, with the chance of a "telling off" whichever way you choose, and the lives of other men hanging in the balance. Suppose you are detailed for a wiring party, and you arrive to find a full moon beaming sardonically down at you. What are you to do? If you go out you may be seen. Half a dozen of your men may be mown down by a machine gun. You will be blamed and will blame yourself for not having decided to remain behind the parapet. If you do not go out you may set a precedent, and night after night the work will be postponed, till at last it is too late, and the Hun has got through, and raided the trench. If you hesitate or ask advice you are lost. You have to make up your mind in aninstant, and to stand by it. If you waver your men will never have confidence in you again.

Still more in a push; a junior subaltern is quite likely to find himself at any time in command of a company, while he may for a day even have to command the relics of a battalion. I have seen boys almost fresh from a Public School in whose faces there were two personalities expressed: the one full of the lighthearted, reckless, irresponsible vitality of boyhood, and the other scarred with the anxious lines of one to whom a couple of hundred exhausted and nerve-shattered men have looked, and not looked in vain, for leadership and strength in their grim extremity. From a boy in such a position is required something far more difficult than personal courage. If we praise the boy soldier for his smile in the face of shells and machine guns, don't let us forget to praise still more the boy officer who, in addition to facing death onhis own account, has to bear the responsibility of the lives of a hundred other men. There is many a man of undoubted courage whose nerve would fail to bear that strain.

A day or two ago I was reading Romance, by Joseph Conrad and Ford Madox Hueffer. It is a glorious tale of piracy and adventure in the West Indies; but for the moment I wondered how it came about that Conrad, the master of psychology, should have helped to write such a book. And then I understood. For these boys who hate the war, and suffer and endure with the smile that is sometimes so difficult, and long with a great longing for home and peace—some day some of them will look back on these days and will tell themselves that after all it was Romance, the adventure, which made their lives worth while. And they will long to feel once again the stirring of the old comradeship and love and loyalty, to dip their clasp-knives into the same pot of jam, andlie in the same dug-out, and work on the same bit of wire with the same machine gun striking secret terror into their hearts, and look into each other's eyes for the same courageous smile. For Romance, after all, is woven of the emotions, especially the elemental ones of love and loyalty and fear and pain.

We men are never content! In the dull routine of normal life we sigh for Romance, and sometimes seek to create it artificially, stimulating spurious passions, plunging into muddy depths in search of it. Now we have got it we sigh for a quiet life. But some day those who have not died will say: "Thank God I have lived! I have loved, and endured, and trembled, and trembling, dared. I have had my Romance."

IMAGINARY CONVERSATIONS

PART I

SCENE. A field in Flanders. All round the edge are bivouacs, built of sticks and waterproof sheets. Three men are squatting round a small fire, waiting for a couple of mess-tins of water to boil.

BILL (gloomily). The last three of the old lot! Oo's turn next?

FRED. Wot's the bleedin' good of bein' dahn in the mahf abaht it? Give me the bleedin' 'ump, you do.

JIM. Are we dahn-'earted? Not 'alf, we ain't!

BILL. I don't know as I cares. Git it over, I sez. 'Ave done wiv it! I dessay as them wot's gone West is better off nor wot we are, arter all.

JIM. Orlright, old sport, you go an' look for the V.C., and we'll pick up the bits an' bury 'em nice an' deep!

BILL. If this 'ere bleedin' war don't finish soon that's wot I bleedin' well will go an' do. Wish they'd get a move on an' finish it.

FRED. If ever I gets 'ome agin, I'll never do another stroke in my natural. The old woman can keep me, —— 'er, an' if she don't I'll—well—'er ——.

JIM (indignantly). Nice sort o' bloke you are! Arter creatin' abaht ole Bill makin' you miserable, you goes on to plan 'ow you'll make other folks miserable! Wot's the bleedin' good o' that? Keep smilin', I sez, an' keep other folks smilin' too, if you can. If ever I gets 'ome I'll go dahn on my bended, I will,and I'll be a different sort o' bloke to wot I been afore. Swelp me, Bob, I will! My missus won't 'ave no cause to wish as I've been done in.

BILL. Ah well, it don't much matter. We're all most like to go afore this war's finished.

JIM. If yer goes yer goes, and that's all abaht it. A bloke's got to go some

41

day, and fer myself I'd as soon get done in doin' my dooty as I would die in my bed. I ain't struck on dyin' afore my time, and I don't know as I'm greatly struck on livin', but, whichever it is, you got ter make the best on it.

BILL (meditatively). I woulden mind stoppin' a bullet fair an' square; but I woulden like one of them 'orrible lingerin' deaths. "Died o' wounds" arter six munfs' mortal hagony—that's wot gets at me. Git it over an' done wiv, I sez.

FRED (querulously). Ow, chuck it, Bill. You gives me the creeps, you do.

JIM. I knowed a bloke onest in civil life wot died a lingerin' death. Lived in the second-floor back in the same 'ouse as me an' my missus, 'e did. Suffered somefink' 'orrible, 'e did, an' lingered more nor five year. Yet I reckon 'e was one o' the best blokes as ever I come acrost. Went to 'eaven straight, 'e did, if ever any one did. Wasn't 'alf glad ter go, neither. "I done my bit of 'ell, Jim," 'e sez to me, an' looked that 'appy you'd a' thought as 'e was well agin. Shan't never forget 'is face, I shan't. An' I'd sooner be that bloke, for all 'is sufferin's, than I'd be old Fred 'ere, an' live to a 'undred.

BILL (philosophically). You'm right, matey. This is a wale o' tears, as the 'ymn sez, and them as is out on it is best off, if so be as they done their dooty in that state o' life.... Where's the corfee, Jim? The water's on the bile.

THE FEAR OF DEATH IN WAR

I am not a psychologist, and I have not seen many people die in their beds; but I think it is established that very few people are afraid of a natural death when it comes to the test. Often they are so weak that they are incapable of emotion. Sometimes they are in such physical pain that death seems a welcome deliverer.

But a violent death such as death in battle is obviously a different matter. It comes to a man when he is in the full possession of his health and vigour, and when every physical instinct is urging him to self-preservation. If a man feared death in such circumstances one could not be surprised, and yet in the present warhundreds of thousands of men have gone to meet practically certain destruction without giving a sign of terror.

The fact is that at the moment of a charge men are in an absolutely abnormal condition.

I do not know how to describe their condition in scientific terms; but there is a sensation of tense excitement combined with a sort of uncanny calm. Their emotions seem to be numbed. Noises, sights, and sensations which would ordinarily produce intense pity, horror, or dread, have no effect on them at all, and yet never was their mind clearer, their sight, hearing, etc., more acute. They notice all sorts of little details which would ordinarily pass them by, but which now thrust themselves on their attention with absurd definiteness—absurd because so utterly incongruous and meaningless. Or they suddenly remember with extraordinary clearness some trivial incident of their past life, hitherto unremembered, and not a bit worthremembering! But with the issue before them, with victory or death or the prospect of eternity, their minds blankly refuse to come to grips.

No; it is not at the moment of a charge that men fear death. As in the case of those who die in bed, Nature has an anesthetic ready for the emergency.

It is before an attack that a man is more liable to fear—before his blood is hot, and while he still has leisure to think. The trouble may begin a day or two in advance, when he is first told of the attack which is likely to mean death to himself and so many of his chums. This part is comparatively easy. It is fairly easy to be philosophic if one has plenty of time. One indulges in regrets about the home one may never see again. One is rather sorry for oneself; but such self-pity is not wholly unpleasant. One feels mildly heroic, which is not wholly disagreeable either. Very few men are afraid of death in the abstract. Very few menbelieve in hell, or are tortured by their consciences. They are doubtful about after-death, hesitating between a belief in eternal oblivion and a belief in a new life under the same management as the present; and neither prospect fills them with terror. If only one's "people" would be sensible, one would not mind.

But as the hour approaches when the attack is due to be launched the strain becomes more tense. The men are probably cooped up in a very small space. Movement is very restricted. Matches must not be struck. Voices must be hushed to a whisper. Shells bursting and machine guns rattling bring home the grim reality of the affair. It is then more than at any other time in an attack that a man has to "face the spectres of the mind," and lay them if he can. Few men care for those hours of waiting.

Of all the hours of dismay that come to a soldier there are really few more trying tothe nerves than when he is sitting in a trench under heavy fire from high-explosive shells or bombs from trench mortars. You can watch these bombs lobbed up into the air. You see them slowly wobble down to earth, there to explode with a terrific detonation that sets every nerve in your body a-jangling. You can do nothing. You cannot retaliate in any way. You simply have to sit tight and hope for the best. Some men joke and smile; but their mirth is forced. Some feign stoical indifference, and sit with a paper and a pipe; but as a rule their pipes are out and their reading a pretence. There are few men, indeed, whose hearts are not beating faster, and whose nerves are not on edge.

But you can't call this "the fear of death"; it is a purely physical reaction of danger and detonation. It is not fear of death as death. It is not fear of hurt as hurt. It is an infinitely intensified dislike of suspense and uncertainty, sudden noiseand shock. It belongs wholly to the physical organism, and the only cure that I know is to make an act of personal dissociation from the behaviour of one's flesh. Your teeth may chatter and your knees quake, but as long as the real you disapproves and derides this absurdity of the flesh, the composite you can carry on. Closely allied to the sensation of nameless dread caused by high explosives is that caused by gas. No one can carry out a relief in the trenches without a certain anxiety and dread if he knows that the enemy has gas cylinders in position and that the wind is in the east. But this, again, is not exactly the fear of death; but much more a physical reaction to uncertainty and suspense combined with the threat of physical suffering.

Personally, I believe that very few men indeed fear death. The vast majority experience a more or less violent physical shrinking from the pain of death andwounds, especially when they are obliged to be physically inactive, and when they have nothing else to think about. This kind of dread is, in the case of a good many men, intensified by darkness and suspense, and by the deafening noise and shock that accompany the detonation of high explosives. But it cannot properly be called the fear of death, and it is a purely physical reaction which can be, and nearly always is, controlled by the mind.

Last of all there is the repulsion and loathing for the whole business of war, with its bloody ruthlessness, its fiendish ingenuity, and its insensate cruelty, that comes to a man after a battle, when the tortured and dismembered dead lie strewn about the trench, and the wounded groan from No-Man's-Land. But neither is that the fear of death. It is a repulsion which breeds hot anger more often than cold fear, reckless hatred of life more often than abject clinging to it.

The cases where any sort of fear, even for a moment, obtains the mastery of a man are very rare. Sometimes in the case of a boy, whose nerves are more sensitive than a man's, and whose habit of self-control is less formed, a sudden shock will upset his mental balance. Sometimes a very egotistical man will succumb to danger long drawn out. The same applies to men who are very introspective. I have seen a man of obviously low intelligence break down on the eve of an attack. The anticipation of danger makes many men "windy," especially officers who are responsible for other lives than their own. But even where men are afraid it is generally not death that they fear. Their fear is a physical and instinctive shrinking from hurt, shock, and the unknown, which instinct obtains the mastery only through surprise, or through the exhaustion of the mind and will, or through a man being excessively self-centred. It is not thefear of death rationally considered; but an irrational physical instinct which all men possess, but which almost all can control.

IMAGINARY CONVERSATIONS

PART II

SCENE. A dug-out in a wood somewhere in Flanders. Officers at tea.

HANCOCK. Damned glad to be out of that infernal firing trench, anyway. (A dull report is heard in the distance.) There goes another torpedo! Wonder who's copt it this time!

SMITH. For Christ's sake talk about something else!

HANCOCK (ignoring him). Are we coming back to the same trenches, sir?

CAPTAIN DODD. 'Spect so.

HANCOCK. At the present rate we shalllast another two spells. I hate this sort of bisnay. You go on month after month losing fellows the whole time, and at the end of it you're exactly where you started. I wish they'd get a move on.

WHISTON. Tired of life?

HANCOCK. If you call this life, yes! If this damned war is going on another two years, I hope to God I don't live to see the end of it.

SMITH. If ever I get home ...!

WHISTON. Well?

SMITH. Won't I paint the town red, that's all!

WHISTON. If ever I get home ... well, I guess I'll go home. No more razzle-dazzle for master! No, there's a little girl awaiting, and I know she thinks of me. Shan't wait any longer.

HANCOCK (heavily). Don't think a chap's got any right to marry a girl under present circs. It's ten to one she's a widow before she's a mother.

SMITH. Oh, shut up!

CAPTAIN DODD (gently). To some women the kid would be just the one thing that made life bearable.

HANCOCK (reddening). Sorry, sir; forgot you'd just done it. Course you're right. Depends absolutely on the girl.

CAPTAIN DODD. Thanks. I say, Whiston, I'm going to B.H.Q. Care to come along?

(They go out together.)

SCENE. A path through a wood. CAPTAIN DODD and WHISTON walking together, followed by a LANCE-CORPORAL.

DODD. D'you believe in presentiments, Whiston?

WHISTON (doubtfully). A year ago I should have laughed at you for asking. Now ...

DODD. More things in heaven and earth ...?

WHISTON. My rationalism is always being upset!

DODD. How exactly?

WHISTON. For instance, I simply can't believe that old John is finished. Can you?

DODD (quietly). No.

WHISTON. Funny thing. As far as I'm concerned I can quite imagine myself just snuffing out. You can put one word on my grave, if I have one—"Napu." But as for John, no. I want something else. Something about Death being scored off after all.

DODD. I know. "O Death, where is thy sting? O Grave, where is thy victory?"

WHISTON. Just that. Mind you, I don't think I'm afraid of Death. I don't want to get killed. But if I saw him coming I think I could smile, and feel that after all he wasn't getting much of a bargain. But the idea of his getting old John sticks in my gullet. I believe inall sorts of things for him. Resurrection and life and Heaven, and all that.

DODD. What do you think about it, Corporal?

LANCE-CORPORAL. Same as Mr. Whiston, sir.

WHISTON. But what about presentiments?

DODD. Oh, I don't know. Funny thing; but all through this fortnight I've been absolutely certain that I was not for it.

LANCE-CORPORAL. Beg pardon, sir, we noticed that, sir!

WHISTON. Well, it's practically over now.

DODD. I'm not so sure. I'm not in a funk, you know. It's simply that I don't feel so sure.

WHISTON. Oh, rot, sir! I don't believe in that sort of presentiment.

DODD. What do you think, Corporal?

LANCE-CORPORAL. I think you goes when your time comes, sir. But it won'tcome to-night, sir. Not after all we been through this spell, and the spell just finished.

DODD. I believe you're right, Corporal. We shall go when our time comes, and not before. I like that idea, you know. It means one hasn't got to worry.

WHISTON. If it means that you go on as you've done the last fortnight, it's a damnable doctrine, sir. You've no business to go taking unnecessary risks simply because you've got bitten by Mohammedanism.

DODD (thoughtfully). You're right, too, Whiston. "Thou shalt not tempt the Lord thy God." One shouldn't take unnecessary risks. Mind you, I don't admit that I have. It just enables one to do one's job with a quiet mind, that's all.

TWO DAYS LATER

SCENE. A billet. HANCOCK and SMITH.

HANCOCK. Damn!

SMITH. What's up? Aren't you satisfied? The brigade's bound to go back and re-form now, and that means that we shan't be in the trenches for a couple of months at least. We may even go where there's a pretty girl or two. My word!

HANCOCK. Damnation!

SMITH (genuinely astonished). What the hell's wrong? Any one would think you liked the trenches! Personally, I don't care if I never see them again. England's full of nice young, bright young things crying to get out. Let 'em all come! They can have my job and welcome!

HANCOCK (to himself). God! Why Dodd and Whiston? Why, why, why? Why not me? Why just the fellows we can't afford to lose?

SMITH. Oh, for God's sake stow it! What the hell's the good of going on like that? Of course I'm sorry for them and all that. But I don't see that it's going to help them to make oneself miserable about it.

HANCOCK (fiercely). Sorry for them! It's not them I'm sorry for! They ... they're the lucky ones! God! I suppose that's the answer! They'd earned it!

SMITH (satirically). Have you turned pi? We shall have you saying the prayers that you learnt at your mother's knee next, I suppose! I shall have to tell the Padre, and he'll preach a sermon about it! I should never have thought you would have been frightened into religion!

HANCOCK. Frightened! You little swine! You talk about being frightened after last night! I tell you I'd rather be lying out there with Dodd and Whiston than be sitting here with you. Frightened into religion!

SMITH. Oh, I suppose you're the next candidate for death or glory! Good luck to you! I'm not competing. I'll do my job; but I'm not going to make a fool of myself. Dodd and Whiston deserved all they got. You're right there. You'll getwhat you deserve some day, I expect! Don't look at me like that. I've said I'm sorry, and all that. But it's the truth I'm speaking, all the same.

HANCOCK. And you'll get what you deserve too, I suppose, which is to live in your own company till the end of your miserable existence. I won't deprive you of your reward more than I can help, I promise you!

(HANCOCK goes out.)

DONALD HANKEY

THE WISDOM OF A STUDENT IN ARMS

It is no good trying to fathom "things" to the bottom; they have not got one.

Knowledge is always descriptive, and never fundamental. We can describe the appearance and conditions of a process; but not the way of it.

Agnosticism is a fundamental fact. It is the starting-point of the wise man who has discovered that it needs eternity to study infinity.

Agnosticism, however, is no excuse for indolence. Because we cannot know all, we need not therefore be totally ignorant.

The true wisdom is that in which all knowledge is subordinate to practical aims,and blended into a working philosophy of life.

The true wisdom is that it is not what a man does, or has, or says, that matters; but what he is.

This must be the aim of practical philosophy—to make a man be something.

The world judges a man by his station, inherited or acquired. God judges by his character. To be our best we must share God's viewpoint.

To the world death is always a tragedy; to the Christian it is never a tragedy unless a man has been a contemptible character.

Religion is the widening of a man's horizon so as to include God.

It is in the nature of a speculation, but its returns are immediate.

True religion means betting one's life that there is a God.

Its immediate fruits are courage, stability, calm, unselfishness, friendship, generosity, humility, and hope.

Religion is the only possible basis of optimism.

Optimism is the essential condition of progress.

One is what one believes oneself to be. If one believes oneself to be an animal one becomes bestial; if one believes oneself spiritual one becomes Divine.

DONALD HANKEY

Faith is an effective force whose measure has never yet been taken.

Man is the creature of heredity and environment. He can only rise superior to circumstances by bringing God into environment of which he is conscious.

The recognition of God's presence upsets the balance of a man's environment, and means a new birth into a new life.

The faculties which perceive God increase with use like any other perceptive faculties.

Belief in God may be an illusion; but it is an illusion that pays.

If belief in God is illusion, happy ishe who is deluded! He gains this world and thinks he will gain the next.

The disbeliever loses this world, and risks losing the next.

To be the centre of one's universe is misery. To have one's universe centred in God is the peace that passeth understanding.

Greatness is founded on inward peace.

Energy is only effective when it springs from deep calm.

The pleasure of life lies in contrasts; the fear of contrasts is a chain that binds most men.

In the hour of danger a man is proven. The boaster hides, and the egotist trembles. He whose care is for others forgets to be afraid.

Men live for eating and drinking, passion and wealth. They die for honour.

Blessed is he of whom it has been said that he so loved giving that he even gave his own life.

IMAGINARY CONVERSATIONS

PART III

SCENE. A trench unpleasantly near the firing line. There has been an hour's intense bombardment by the British, with suitable retaliation by the Boches. The retaliation is just dying down.

CHARACTERS. ALBERT—Round-eyed, rotund, red-cheeked, yellow-haired, and deliberate; in civil life probably a drayman. JIM—Small, lean, sallow, grey-eyed, with a kind of quiet restlessness; in civil life probably a mechanic with leanings towards Socialism. POZZIE—A thick-set, low-browed, impassive, silentcountry youth, with a face the colour of the soil. JINKS—An old soldier, red, lean, wrinkled, with very blue eyes. His face is rough-hewn, almost grotesque like a gargoyle. In his eyes there is a perpetual glint of humour, and in the poise of his head a certain irrepressible jauntiness.

ALBERT (whose eyes are more staring than ever, his cheeks pendulous and crimson, his general air that of a partly deflated air-cushion). Gawd's truth!

JINKS (wagging his head). Well, my old sprig o' mint, what's wrong wi' you?

ALBERT. It ain't right. (Sententiously) It's agin natur'. Flesh an' blood weren't made for this sort o' think.

JIM. It ain't flesh an' blood that can't stand it. It's Mind. Look at old Pozzie. 'E's flesh an' blood, and don't turn an 'air! For myself I'll go potty one o' these days.

JINKS (slapping POZZIE on the back). You don't take no notice, do you, old lump o' duff?

POZZIE. Oi woulden moind if I got moy rations; but a chap can't keep a good 'eart if 'e's got an empty stummick.

JIM (sarcastically). You keep yer 'eart in yer stomach, don't yer? You ain't got no mind, you ain't. Jinks was born potty, an' the rest of us'll all go potty except you. It's you an' yer Ally Sloper's Cavalry what'll win the war, I don't think!

ALBERT. What I wants ter know is 'ow long the bleedin' war's a-goin' ter last. If it goes on much longer I'll be potty if I ain't a gone 'un.

JIM. There's only one way of ending it as I knows on.

ALBERT. What's that, matey?

JIM. Put all the bleedin' politicians on both sides in the bleedin' trenches. Give 'em a week's bombardment, an'send 'em away for a week to make peace, with a promise of a fortnight's intense at. the end of it if they've failed. They'd find a way, sure enough.

ALBERT (admiringly). Ah, that they would an' all. If old "Wait and See" 'ad been 'ere these last four days 'e wouldn't talk about fightin' to the last man!

JINKS. Don't talk stoopid. 'Oo began the bloomin' war? Don't yer know what you're fightin' for? D'you want ter leave the 'Uns in France an' Belgium an' Serbia an' all? It ain't fer us to make peace. It's fer the 'Uns. An' if you are done in, you got to go under some day. I ain't sure as they ain't the lucky ones what's got it over and done with. And arter all, it's not us what's not proper. The 'Uns 'ave 'ad two fer our one.

ALBERT. They got dug-outs as deep as 'ell, it don't touch 'em.

JINKS. (but without conviction). Don't talk silly.

POZZIE. Oi reckon we got to go through with it. But they didn't ought to give a chap short rations. That's what takes the 'eart out of a chap.

LETTER TO AN ARMY CHAPLAIN

April 17, 1916.

Letter to an army chaplain2

Thank you very much for your letter of a week ago, which I should have tried to answer before if I had had time. I am afraid that your confidence in me as an oracle will be severely shaken when I confess that I was once on the eve of being ordained, and that in the end I funked it because it seemed such an awfully difficult job, and I couldn't see my way to going through with it.

However, I must try to answer yourletter as best I can, and I hope that you will not mind my speaking plainly what I think, and will remember that I do so in no spirit of superiority, but very humbly, as one who has funked the great work that you have had the pluck to take up, and who has even failed in the little bit of work that he himself did try and do. This last means that I have no business to be an officer. It was the biggest mistake in my life, for my position in the ranks did give me a hold on the fellows, the strength of which I have only realized since I left.

Now then to the point. As I understand you, your difficulty is that you feel that you must devote yourself to strengthening a very few men who are already Churchmen, and to whom you can talk in the language of the Church of things which you know they want to hear about, or you must appeal to the crowd of those who are merely good fellowsand often sad scamps too, who must be caught with buns and cinemas and who are very difficult to get any farther.

I fancy that you, like me, when you see a fine dashing young fellow, with a touch of honesty and recklessness and wonderful mystery of youth in his eyes, love him as a brother, and long to do something to keep him clean, and to keep him from the sordid things to which you and I know well enough he will descend in the long run if one cannot put the love of clean, wholesome life into his heart. But how to get at him? If you talk to him about his soul you disgust him, and you feel a sort of sneaking sympathy with him too. It does not seem the thing to make a chap self-conscious and a bit of a prig when he is not one to start with. On the other hand, if you just keep to buns and cinemas you never get any farther. Well, it is a big difficulty. The only experience that I have had which counts at all is experiencethat I gained while trying to run a boys' club in South London, and you must not think me egotistical if I tell you what seems to me to have been the secret of any power that I seem to have had over fellows.

At first I used to have a short service at the close of the club every evening, to which most of the boys used to stay. I also had a service on Sunday afternoon. Something of the same sort might perhaps be possible in the Y.M.C.A. tent if there is one where you are. When I was talking to them at these services I always used to try and make them feel that Christ was the fulfilment of all the best things that they admired, that He was their natural hero. I would tell them some story of heroism and meanness contrasted, of courage and cowardice, of noble forgiveness and vile cruelty, and so get them on the side of the angels. Then I would try and spring it upon them that Christ was the Lord of the heroes and the bravemen and the noble men, and that He was fighting against all that was mean and cruel and cowardly, and that it was up to them to take their stand by His side if they wanted to make the world a little better instead of a little worse, and I would try to show them how in little practical ways in their homes and at their work and in the club they could do a bit for Christ.

Well, they listened pretty well, and I think that they agreed in a general sort of way, only 'they knew that I was a richish man in comparison with them, and that I didn't have their difficulties to contend with, and that all tended to undo the effect of what I had said. And then accident gave me a sort of clue to the way to get them to take one seriously. For some idiotic reason— I really couldn't say just what it was—I dressed up as a tramp one day, and spent a night in a casual ward. I didn't do it for any very worthy motive, and I didn't mean anyone to know about it; but it got round, and I suddenly found that it had caught the imaginations of some of the fellows, and I realized that if one was to have any power over them one must do symbolic things to show them that one meant what one said about love being really better than money, and all that sort of thing. So in rather a half-hearted way I did try to do things which would show them that I was in earnest. I took a couple of rooms in a little cottage in a funny little bug-ridden court, instead of living at the mission-house. I went out to Australia steerage to see why emigration of London boys was not a success, and when war broke out I enlisted, although I had previously held a commission. And all these little

A STUDENT IN ARMS

things, though on reasonable grounds often rather indefensible, undoubtedly had the effect of making my South London boys take me more seriously than they did at first. Well, I am quite sure that with Tommies, ifever you get a chance of doing something in the way of sharing their privations and dangers when you aren't obliged to, or of showing in practical ways humility and unselfishness, that will endear you to them, and give you weight with them more than anything else. In my time in the ranks I had that proved over and over again. If once I was able to do even a small kindness for a fellow which involved a bit of unnecessary trouble, he would never forget it, and would repay me a thousand times over. I was a sergeant for about nine months in England, and had one or two chances. Then I reverted to the ranks, and for that the men could not do enough to show me kindness. (It was my not valuing rank and comparative comfort for its own sake that appealed to them.) Continually I have reaped a most gigantic reward of goodwill for actions which cost very little, and which were not always done from the motives imputed.

I am not swanking—at least, I don't mean to—but that is just my experience, that with Tommy it is actions, and specially actions that imply and symbolize humility, courage, unselfishness, etc., that count ten thousand times more than the best sermons in the world. I am afraid that all this is not much good because you are an officer, and your course of action is very clearly marked out for you by authority. But I do say that if ever you have a chance of showing that you are willing to share the often hard and sometimes humiliating lot of the men it is that which above all things will give you power with them; just as it is the Cross of Christ, and the spitting and the mocking and the scourging, and the degradation of His exposure in dying, that gives Him His power far more than even the Sermon on the Mount. After all, it is always what costs most that is best worth having, and if you only see Tommyin his easiest moments, when he is at the Y.M.C.A. or the club, you see him at the time when he is least impressionable in a permanent manner.

Well, I must apologize for writing such an egotistical and intimate sort of letter on so slight a provocation. But this that I have said is all that my experience has taught me about influencing the Tommy.

No doubt there are other ways; but I have not been able to strike them.

Yours very truly,

DONALD HANKEY, 2nd Lieut.

P.S.—Of course in becoming a Second Lieutenant I have dished my own influence most effectually. It has often appeared to me that among ordinary working men humility was considered the Christian virtue par excellence. Humility combined with love is so rare, I suppose, and that is why it is marvelled at.

Footnote 2:

DONALD HANKEY

This chapter is the actual text of a letter from "A Student in Arms," and like the most of the other chapters appeared originally in the Spectator.

DON'T WORRY

This is at present the soldier's favourite chorus at the front—
"What's the use of worrying?
It never was worth while!
Pack up your troubles in your old kit-bag
And Smile, Smile, Smile!"
Not a bad chorus, either, for the trenches! You can't stop a shell from bursting in your trench, even if Mr. Rawson can! You can't stop the rain, or prevent a light from going up just as you are half-way over the parapet ... so what on earth is the use of worrying? If you can't alter things, you must accept them, and make the best of them.
Yet some men do worry, and by so doing effectually destroy their peace of mind without doing any one any good. What is worse, it is often the religious man who worries. I have even heard those whose care was for the soldier's soul, deplore the fact that he did not worry! I have heard it said that the soldier is so careless, realizes his position so little, is so hard to touch! And, on the other hand, I have heard the soldier say that he did not want religion, because it would make him worry. Strange, isn't it, if Christianity means worry and anxiety, and if it is only the heathen who is cheerful and free from care? Yet the feeling that this is so undoubtedly exists, and it must have some foundation. Perhaps it is one of the subjects which ought to engage the attention of Churchmen in these days of "repentance and hope."
Of course, worrying is about as un-Christian as anything can be. "μη μεριμνατετη ψυχη υμων"—"Don't worry about your life"—is the Master's express command. In fact, the call of Christ is a call to something very like the cheerfulness of the soldier in the trenches. It is a call to a life of external turmoil and internal peace. "I came not to bring peace, but a sword"; "take

up your cross and follow Me"; "ye shall be hated"; "he that would save his life shall lose it." It is a call to take risks, to risk poverty, unpopularity, humiliation, death. It is a call to follow the way of the Cross. But the way of the Cross is also the way of peace, the peace of God that passeth understanding. It is a way of freedom from all cares, and anxieties, and fears; but not a way of escape from them.

Yet worrying is often a feature of the actual Churchman. The actual Churchman is often a man whose conscience is an incubus. He can do nothing without weighing motives and calculating results.It makes him introspective to an extent that is positively morbid. He is continually probing himself to discover whether his motives are really pure and disinterested, continually trying to decide whether he is "worthy" or "fit" to undertake this or that responsibility, or to face this or that eventuality. He is full of suspicion of himself, of self-distrust. In the trenches he is always wondering whether he is fit to die, whether he will acquit himself worthily in a crisis, whether he has done anything that he ought not to have done, or left undone anything that he ought to have done. Especially if he is an officer, his responsibility weighs on him terribly, and I have known more than one good fellow and conscientious Churchman worry himself into thinking that he was unfit for his responsibilities as an officer, and ask to be relieved of them.

There must be something wrong about the Christianity of such men. Theirover-conscientiousness seems to create a wholly wrong sense of proportion, an exaggerated sense of the significance of their own actions and characters which is as far removed as can be from the childlike humility which Christ taught. The truth seems to be that we lay far too much stress on conscience, self-examination, and personal salvation, and that we trust the Holy Spirit far too little.

If we look to the teaching of Christ, we do not find any recommendation to meticulous self-analysis, but rather we are taught a kind of spiritual recklessness, an unquestioning confidence in what seem to be right impulses, and that quite regardless of results. We are not told to be careful to spend each penny to the best advantage; but we are told that if our money is preventing us from entering the Kingdom, we had better give it all away. We are not told to set a high value on our lives, and to spend them with care for the good of theKingdom. On the contrary, we are told to risk our lives recklessly if we would preserve them. A sense of anxious responsibility is discouraged. If our limbs cause us to offend, we are advised to cut them off.

The whole teaching of the Gospels is that we have got to find freedom and peace in trusting ourselves implicitly to the care of God. We have got to follow what we think right quite recklessly, and leave the issue to God; and in judging between right and wrong we are only given two rules for our guidance. Everything which shows love for God and love for man is right, and everything which shows personal ambition and anxiety is wrong.

What all this means as far as the trenches are concerned is extraordinarily clear. The Christian is advised not to be too pushing or ambitious. He is advised to "take the lowest room." But if he is told to move up higher, he has got to go. If he is givenresponsibility, there is no question of refusing it. He has got to do his best and leave the issue to God. If he does well, he will be given more responsibility. But there is no need to worry. The same formula holds good for the new sphere. Let him do his best and leave the issue to God. If he does badly, well, if he did his best, that means that he was not fit for the job, and he must be perfectly willing to take a humbler job, and do his best at that.

As for personal danger, he must not think of it. If he is killed, that is a sign that he is no longer indispensable. Perhaps he is wanted elsewhere. The enemy can only kill the body, and the body is not the important thing about him. Every man who goes to war must, if he is to be happy, give his body, a living sacrifice, to God and his country. It is no longer his. He need not worry about it. The peace of God which passeth all understanding simply comes from not worrying about resultsbecause they are God's business and not ours, and in trusting implicitly all impulses that make for love of God and man. Few of us perhaps will ever attain to a full measure of such faith; but at least we can make sure that our "Christianity" brings us nearer to it.

IMAGINARY CONVERSATIONS

PART IV

AU COIFFEUR

SCENE. A barber's shop in a small French town about thirty miles from the front. A SUBALTERN and a stout BOURGEOIS are waiting their turn.

BOURGEOIS. Is it that it is the mud of the trenches on the boots of Monsieur?

SUBALTERN. Ah! but no, Monsieur, for then it would reach to my waist!

BOURGEOIS. Nevertheless, Monsieur is but recently come from the trenches, is it not so?

SUBALTERN. Yes, I am arrived from the trenches yesterday.

BOURGEOIS. Then Monsieur has assisted at the great attack!

SUBALTERN. Oh, yes, I helped a very little bit.

BOURGEOIS. There have been immense losses, is it not so?

SUBALTERN (vaguely). There are always great losses when one attacks.

BOURGEOIS. Ah! but much greater than one expected—I have seen, I, the wounded coming down the river.

SUBALTERN. I—I have always expected great losses.

BOURGEOIS. 'Tis true. There are always great losses when one attacks. But all goes well, Monsieur, is it not so?

SUBALTERN. It is difficult to estimate the success of an attack until after several weeks. But I think that all goes well.

BOURGEOIS. But yes, the French, they have had a great success, and also theEnglish. The English are wonderful. Their equipment! It is that which astonishes me. Everything is complete. They say that the English have saved France; but the French also, they have saved England, is it not so,

63

Monsieur?

SUBALTERN. But we are saving each other!

BOURGEOIS. Good! We are saving each other! Very good! But after the war, Monsieur, England will fight against France, hein?

SUBALTERN. Never!

BOURGEOIS. Never?

SUBALTERN. Never in life!

BOURGEOIS. You think so?

SUBALTERN. We do not love war. We do not seek war. It is only when a nation is so execrable that one is compelled to fight, as have been the Germans, that we make war.

BOURGEOIS. You do not love war, eh? Before the war you had a very small Army,about three hundred thousand, is it not so? And now you have about three million. You do not love war, you others.

SUBALTERN. The Germans thought that they loved war, but I do not believe that they will love it very much longer!

BOURGEOIS. No! The war will give them the stomach-ache. They will love it no longer!

COIFFEUR. But these English, whom did they fight before? The Boers, was it not?

SUBALTERN. Yes, but a great many English think now that it was a bêtise. There was also great provocation. And nevertheless, who knows if there was not in that affair also a German plot?

BOURGEOIS. It is very likely. Then Monsieur thinks that we are true friends, the English and the French?

SUBALTERN. But yes, Monsieur, because we love, both of us, liberty and peace.

A PASSING IN JUNE 1915

PROLOGUE

SCENE. The parlour of an Auberge.
PERSONS. A stoist motherly MADAME, a wrinkled fatherly MONSIEUR, and a plain but pleasant MA'MSELLE. Some English soldiers drinking. CECIL is talking in French to MONSIEUR, and they are all very friendly.
MADAME. Alors, vous n'avez pas encore été aux tranchées?
CECIL. Mais non, Madame, peut-être ce soir.
(MONSIEUR and MADAME exchange glances. CECIL rises to go.)
CECIL. À Jeudi, Monsieur, Madame, Ma'mselle.
MONSIEUR, MADAME, AND MA'MSELLE (in chorus). À Jeudi, Monsieur.
MADAME (earnestly). Bon courage, Monsieur!
(Curtain)

ACT I. DAWN

CECIL is discovered lying behind a wall of sandbags. On one side are the sandbags, and on the other an idyllic spring scene, with flowers and orchards seen in the half-light of a spring morning. The dawn breaks gently, and soon bullets begin to ping through the air, flattening themselves against the sandbags, or passing over CECIL's head. He wakes and yawns, and then composes himself with his eyes open.
Enter Allegorical personages: FATHER SUN, MOTHER EARTH, and a chorus of GRASSES, POPPIES, CORNFLOWERS, RAGGED ROBINS, DAISIES, BEETLES, BEES, FLIES, and insects of all kinds.

FATHER SUN.
Wake, children, rub your eyes,
Up and dance and sing and play,
Not a cloud is in the skies;
This is going to be my day.
See the tiny dew-drop glisten
In my glancing golden ray;
See the shadows dancing, listen
To the lark so blithe and gay.
Up, children, dance and play,
This is my own festal day.
FLOWERS, BEETLES, ETC.
Dance and sing
In a ring,
Naughty clouds are chased away;
Oh what fun,
Father Sun
Is going to shine the whole long day.
MOTHER EARTH. That's right, children. This is the day to grow in; but
don't forget to come home to dinner; I've got such a nice dinner for you.
(The children dance away delightedly, while CECIL watches them,
fascinated.)
MOTHER EARTH. What's this absurd young man doing, sitting behind
that ugly wall? Why don't he sit under a tree if he must sit?
FATHER SUN. Oh, he's a lunatic! Must be.
(RANDOM BULLET jumps over the sandbags into the dug-out, and
jibbers impotently at CECIL, who glances up at him with a look of disgust.)
RANDOM BULLET. Ping! Ping. It's me he's afraid of. He daren't stir a
yard from this wall, or I'd tear his brains out. Ping! Ping!
MOTHER EARTH. Who are you, Monster?
RANDOM BULLET. I'm Random Bullet. I am a monster, I am! Ping!
MOTHER EARTH. Who sent you, anyway?
RANDOM BULLET. Why, the idiots behind the other wall, over there!
Sometimes I jump at them, and sometimes I jump over here. I don't care
which way it is; but I like tearing their brains out, I do. I don't care which
lot it is.
MOTHER EARTH. What madness!
FATHER SUN (indignantly). On my day too!
RANDOM BULLET. Mad! I should think they were! Never mind, they
give me some fun! Ping! So long, I'm off, going to jump at the other
fellows, back in a second if you like to wait.
(RANDOM BULLET jumps out of sight, and MOTHER EARTH and
FATHER SUN move disgustedly away.)

CECIL (getting up). Mad! By God, we are mad! Curse the war! Curse the fools who started it! Why did I ever come out here? What a way to spend a morning in June!
(Curtain.)

ACT II. MIDDAY

SCENE. The same. CECIL as before, but sweltering in the sun. Enter the SPIRIT OF THIRST.

THIRST. Oh for a drink! Water, anything! I could drink a bath full. What a place to spend a June day in! When one thinks of all the drinks one might be having, it is really infuriating. Gad! The very thought of 'em makes me feel quite poetic! Think of the great barrels of still cider in cool Devonshire cellars! Think of the sour refreshing wine we usedto get in Italy! And the iced cocktails of Colombo! And Pimm's No. 1 in the City. Anywhere but here it's a pleasure to be a Thirst; but here! Good Lord, it will send me off my head. How would a bath go now, old chap? By God, don't you wish you were back in your canoe, drawn up among the rushes near Islip, and you just going to plunge into the cool waters of the Char? Or think of that day you bathed in the deep still pool at the foot of the Tamarin Falls, with the water crashing down above you, into the deep shady chasm. Even a dip in the sea at Mount Lavinia wouldn't be bad now,—or, better still, a dive into Como from a rowboat; you remember that hot summer we went to Como? I'll tell you another thing that wouldn't go down badly either. Do you remember a great bowl of strawberries and cream with a huge ice in it, that you had the day before you left school, after that hot bike ride to Leamington? Not bad, was it?

CECIL (fiercely). Shut up, you beast! Oh, curse this idiotic war! Why are we such fools?
(Curtain.)

ACT III. LATE AFTERNOON

SCENE. As before. CECIL is discovered reading a letter from home.

CECIL (to himself). Tom dead. Good Lord! What times we have had together! Where are all the good fellows I used to know? Half of them dead, and the rest condemned to die! No more yachting on the broads! No more convivial evenings at the Troc.! No more long nights spinning yarns in Tom's old rooms in the Temple! Curse this blasted war that robs one of everything worth having, that dulls every sense of decency and kills all feeling for beauty, destroys the joy of life, and mutilates one's dearest friends. Curse it!

(A sound as of an express train is heard, followed by the roar of an explosion, while a dense cloud of smoke and dust rises immediately in view of the trench.)

PORTENTOUS VOICE. Prepare to face eternity!

CECIL (clenching his fists). Beast, loathsome beast! Don't think I am afraid of you.

(The sounds are repeated as a second shell drops, rather nearer. A Shadow appears round the dug-out, and hesitates.)

CECIL (to the Shadow). Who is that? Is that the Shadow of Fear?

A THIN, QUAVERING VOICE. Yes, shall I come in?

CECIL (furiously). Out of my sight, vile, cringing wretch! Not even your shadow will I tolerate in my presence!

(A third shell bursts nearer still.)

PORTENTOUS VOICE (thunderously). Set not your affections on things below.

(CECIL pauses in a listening attitude).

CECIL (more quietly, and with a new look in his eyes). I think I have forgotten something,—something rather important.

(Enter the twin Spirits of HONOUR and DUTY, Spirits of a very noble and courtly mien.)

CECIL (simply and humbly). Gentlemen, to my sorrow and loss I had forgotten you. You are doubly welcome.

THE SPIRIT OF DUTY. Young sir, we thank you. After all, it is but right that in this hour of danger and dismay we should be with you.

THE SPIRIT OF HONOUR. I am so old a friend of you and yours, Cecil, that you may surely trust me. I was your father's friend. Side by side we stood in every crisis of his varied life. Togetherfaced the Dervish rush at Abu Klea, and afterwards in India took our part in many a desperate unnamed frontier tussle. I helped him woo your mother, spoke for him when he put up for Parliament, advised him when he visited the city. In fact, I was his companion all through life, and I stood beside his bed at death.

THE SPIRIT OF DUTY. I too may claim to have been as much your father's friend as was my brother. Indeed, where one is, the other is never far away. We do agree most wonderfully, and since our birth, no quarrel has ever disturbed the harmony of our ways.

CECIL. Gentlemen, you have recalled me to myself. I had forgotten that I was no more a child. I wanted to dance in the sun with the flowers, and sing with the birds, to swim in the pool with yonder newt, and lie down to dry in the long meadow grass among the poppies. Because I might not do this and other things as fondand foolish, I was petulant and peevish, like a spoilt child. I look to you, gentlemen, to help me to be a man, and play a man's part in the world.

HONOUR. We will remain at hand, call us when you need us, we shall not

A STUDENT IN ARMS

fail you.

(The bombardment increases in intensity. Shrapnel bursts overhead. Shells with increasing rapidity and accuracy explode both short and over the trench. The hail of bullets is continuous. An N.C.O. rushes by shouting "Stand to"; men rush from the dug-outs and seize their rifles; CECIL, like the others, grasps his rifle and sees that it is fully loaded.)

(Curtain.)

ACT IV. SUNSET

SCENE. The same, but the wall of sand-bags bags is broken in many places. The dead lie half-buried beneath them. CECIL lies, badly wounded, against a gap in the wall, his rifle by his side. HONOUR and DUTY kneel beside him tenderly. The last rays of the sun light up his painful smile. THIRST stands gloomily over him, and the wild flowers are peeping at him with sleepy eyes through the gap, while MOTHER EARTH calls to them to go to bed. FATHER SUN leans sadly over the broken parapet.

CECIL (slowly and with difficulty). Honour, Duty, I thank you. You did not fail me.

HONOUR. You played the man, Cecil, as your father did before you.

DUTY. Your example it was that steadied your comrades, and kept craven fear at a distance. You saved the trench.

HONOUR. This is the beauty of manhood, to die for a good cause. There is no fairer thing in all God's world.

CECIL. I thank you. Good-night, Sun; good-night, Mother Earth. Think kindly of me. I don't think I was mad after all.

SUN. Good-night, brave lad. (To MOTHER EARTH) I can hardly bear to look on so sad a sight.

CECIL. Good-night, Ragged Robins; good-night, Poppies. You have played your game, and I mine. Only they are different because we are different.

CHORUS OF FLOWERS. Good-night, dear Cecil. We are so very sorry that you are hurt.

(Enter the MASTER, flowers shyly following him. HONOUR and DUTY raise CECIL gently to a standing position.)

THE MASTER (extending his arms with a loving smile). "Well done, good and faithfulservant. Enter thou into the joy of thy Lord."

(CECIL, with a look of wonder and joy, is borne forward.)

(Curtain.)

MY HOME AND SCHOOL

My home and school3
A Fragment of Autobiography

CHAPTER I. MY HOME

What is one to say of home? It is difficult to know. I find that biographers are particular about the date of birth, the exact address of the babe, the social position and ancestry of the parent. I suppose that it is all that they can learn. But as an autobiographer I want to do something better; to give a picture of the home where, as I can now see, ideals, tastes, prejudices and habits were formed which havepersisted through all the internal revolutions that have since upheaved my being.

I try to form the picture in my mind, and a crowd of detail rushes in which completely destroys its simplicity and harmony. How hard it is to judge, even at this distance, what are the salient features. I must try, but I know that from the point of view of psychological development I may easily miss out the very factors which were really most important.

I remember a big house, in a row of other big houses, in a side street leading from the East Cliff at Brighton right up to the edge of the bare rolling downs. It was exactly like almost every other house in that part of Brighton—stucco fronted, with four stories and a basement, three windows in front on each of the upper stories, and two windows and a door on the ground floor and basement. At the back was a small garden, with flower beds surrounding a square of gravel, and atricycle house in one corner. There was a back door in this garden, which gave on to a street of cottages. This back door was a point of strategic importance.

But I need not describe the house in detail. It was exactly like thousands of other houses built in the beginning of the nineteenth century. High, respectable, ugly and rather inconvenient, with many stairs, two or three big rooms, a lot of small ones and no bathroom. It was essentially a family house, intended for people of moderate means and large families. Nowadays they build houses which are prettier, and have bathrooms; but they are not meant for large families.

We were a large family, and a fairly noisy one. Moreover, we were singularly self-sufficing. We hadn't many friends, we didn't entertain much, we had dinner in the middle of the day, and supper in the evening.

There was my father who was a recluse,my mother who was essentially our mother, the two girls and four boys. I was an afterthought, being seven years younger than my next brother, who for seven years had been called B. (for baby), and couldn't escape from it even after my appearance.

In addition to these, B. and I both had inseparable friends, who lived within a stone's throw. Ronnie was my alter ego till I was fourteen: so much so that I had no other friend. Even now, though our ways have kept us apart, and our interests and opinions are fundamentally different, we can sit in each other's rooms with perfect content. We know too much of each other for it to be possible to pretend to be what we are not. We sit and are ourselves, naked and unashamed so to speak, and it is very restful.

Pictures float before my mind. Let me select a few. I see a rather fat, stolid little boy in a big airy nursery at the top of the house, sitting in the middle of thefloor playing with bricks. Outside it is gusty and wet, and the small boy hopes that he will be allowed to stay in all the afternoon, and play with bricks. But that is not to be. A small thin man, with gentle grey eyes, short curly beard, an old black greatcoat and a black square felt hat, comes in. The child must have some air. The child is resentful, but resigned, is wrapped up well, put in his pram and wheeled up and down the Madeira Road.

"Pa" didn't appear very much except on some such errand; but "Ma" was in and out all the time. "Ma" was everything, the only woman who has ever had my whole love, my whole trust and has made my heart ache with the desire to show my love.

A later picture. The boy is bigger, and not so fat. He no longer has a nurse. He has vacated the nursery, which is now tenanted by his big sisters. He has a little room all his own: a very small room,looking west. The south-west gales beat upon the window in the winter, and not so far away is the roar of the sea. It is good to curl up in a nice warm little bed, and listen to the howling of the wind and the waves.

In the morning come lessons from his eldest sister G. The schoolroom has rings and a trapeze, a bookshelf full of boys' books, and cupboards full of stone bricks, cannon and soldiers. The boy's mind is set on bricks and soldiers. Lessons and walks with "Ma" and his sisters or Ronnie and his nurse down the town are a nuisance. They interfere with the building of cathedrals and the settling of the destinies of nations by the arbitrament of war.

It was a stolid, placid boy, intensely wrapt up in his cathedrals and his generals, intensely devoted to "Ma," and regarding all else as rather a

A STUDENT IN ARMS

nuisance. Ronnie he liked. He liked going to tea with him, and going walks with him and hisnurse; but they didn't have much in common except cricket. Ronnie had big soldiers which could not be knocked down by cannon balls, and which couldn't make history because they were few in number, and nearly all English. Mine were of every European power, and many Asiatic ones. They were diminutive and numerous, could take shelter in a forest of pine cones and were admirably suited to be mown down at the cannon's mouth. The King of England was a person with a fine figure. He had one leg and one arm, and the plume of his dragoon's helmet was shorn off; but his slight, erect figure still looked noble on a stately white palfrey. The French armies were usually commanded by Marshal Petit, a gay fellow with his full complement of limbs, who sat a horse well. He had a younger brother almost equally distinguished. I have no recollection of a King of France. He must have been a poor fellow. The Sultan of Turkey, the Khedive,and Li Hung Chang still live in my memory as persons of distinction; but I have no personal recollection of the Tsar, or the Emperors of Germany or Austria, or of the King of Italy, though I know they existed.

Into this placid existence turmoil would enter three times a year. The elder brothers, Hugh, Tommy and B., would come home for the holidays from Sandhurst and Rugby, and R. would appear, and become almost one of the family. Then would occur troublous times, with a few advantages and many disadvantages.

"Tommy" was a curiously solitary youth as I remember him, who played the 'cello with great perseverance and considerable success. At soldiers he was something of a genius, though his games were of an intricacy which failed to commend itself to me altogether. In his great soldier days he not only made history, but wrote it—a height to which I never attained.

In the holidays, cricket in the back garden became a great feature, and Tommy was a demon bowler. I fancy, too, that the very elaborate but highly satisfactory form of the game must have originated with him. In the back garden we not merely played cricket, but made history—cricket history. Two county sides were written out, and we batted alternately for the various cricketers, doing our best to imitate their styles. We bowled also in a rough imitation of the styles of the county bowlers whom we represented. This arrangement secured us against personal rivalry, kept up a tremendous interest in first-class cricket and enabled matches to continue, if necessary, for weeks at a time. It encouraged, too, a fair, impersonal and unprejudiced view of outside events.

In cricket, war and music we undoubtedly benefited by the holidays, especially in the summer, when we used to go to the country, often occupying a school-housewith gym, cricket nets and a fair-sized garden. Ecclesiastical architecture suffered, however....

Hugh was a great and glorious person, a towering beneficent despot when he did appear.... As for me I adored him with whole-hearted hero-worship. He was the "protector of the poor," who kept the rest of us in order. He was a magnificent person who revolutionized the art of war by the introduction of explosives. He was a tremendous walker, and first taught me to love great tramps over the downs, to sniff appreciatively the glorious air and to love their bare, storm-swept outlines. Hugh stood for all that is wholesome, strenuous, out of doors in my life. Without him I should have been a mere sedentary. Among other things he was an enthusiastic boxer and gymnast. For these pursuits I sturdily feigned enthusiasm and suppressed timidity.

A few more pictures. First, Sundaymorning. Gertrude goes off to Sunday School. She likes teaching and bossing. Hilda and Hugh, who are greater pals than brother and sister can often be, go off to St. James', where there will be good music and an interesting sermon. Tommy goes to St. Mark's, a good Protestant place, or to the beach, where curious and recondite doctrines are weekly disputed. B. goes to St. George's, protesting. There is plenty of room for his hat, there is a congenially aggressive spirit against Rome and it slightly irritates Ma. Pa is not up yet. Ma and I go to All Souls', because it is the nearest poor church, and Ma finds it easier to worship where there are no pew rents, and the seats are uncushioned, and there are few rich people. I am ever loyal to Ma.

I often wonder whether the reason why my family are all Churchgoers now is not that at that time we could choose our church.

The next picture is Sunday night. "Pa" and I, and perhaps some of the other boys, set out for St. Paul's, at the other end of the town. Then, after the service, follows an immense walk all through the slums of the town. We talk of Australia, where Pa once had a sheep run; of theology, of the past and the future. This weekly walk is something of a privilege, and rather solemn. It makes me feel older.

It is spring. I am at Rugby, and in the "San" with ophthalmia. The South African war is raging. Hugh is there. I am told that Hugh is dead. He has been shot in a glorious but futile charge at Paardeberg. I can't realize it. I am an object of interest, of envy almost, to the whole school. The flag is half-mast because my brother is dead. Every one is kind, touched. I put on an air as of a martyr.

I get a heartbroken letter from my mother. Will I come home? Or hadn'tI better go to Uncle Jack's? If I go home we shall make each other worse. It is better for me than for Maurice, who is with the fleet in the Mediterranean with no one to comfort him.

Ma has had a great shock. She feels it desperately. She thinks all the others feel it as much. Except Hilda, we don't. There is a huge piece taken out of Ma's life and Hilda's life, because they were so unselfishly devoted to Hugh.

A STUDENT IN ARMS

Pa, also, has lost much, but he is a philosopher.

I go to Uncle Jack's and shoot rabbits. The holidays come and go. Tommy is at Oxford; I am at Rugby. Pa is immersed in theological speculation about the next world; B. is in the Mediterranean. Ma sends Gertrude and Hilda away for a long change. They go, and come back. Something about Ma frightens them. She and Pa come near Rugby and stay with Uncle Jack. The holidays come. I learn that for the first time for about twenty years Ma is to go away without Pa. I am to meet her at Hereford, and we are to go to Wales. Ma forgets things. She is more loving than ever, but her memory is going. We go to communion together in the little village church.

A few weeks later. We are back in Brighton. An Australian uncle and family are staying with us. Ma is ill in bed. I get up at 6 A.M., tramp over the downs and in a place I wot of, some five miles away, I gather heather for Ma. I run. I get back by 8.30. I find my uncle and cousins getting into a cab. Some one says, "How lovely! Are these for me?" I grip them in despair. They are for Ma. "Quite right," says someone. A day or two later my heather was placed, still blooming, on Ma's grave.

I was sixteen then. Six years later I return home from abroad. Within a few weeks of my return I am sitting in Pa's room in agony, listening to him fight for breath. The fight at last weakens. Ihear him whisper, "Help! help!" I set my teeth. The others come in. There is silence. All is over. I am given my father's ring. It is my most treasured possession.

Henceforth all I have left of home is Hilda, for she alone is unmarried. Ever since my mother's death she has been my confidante. As far as was possible she has taken Ma's place in my life, and I have taken Hugh's place in hers. We are substitutes. For that reason as we get older we get to know each other better, and to know better how much we can give to each other. There is more criticism between us than there would have been between Ma and me, and Hilda and Hugh. But it has its advantages. We live apart, but we correspond weekly, and holiday together. It is all that is left of home, and it is infinitely precious.

Now that I have written these pages I can see as I have never seen before how much the child was father of the man.Since those home days I have had more variety of experience perhaps than falls to the lot of most men, and I would almost say more varied and more epoch-making friendships. Yet in these pages that I have written I seem to see all the essential and salient features of my character already mirrored and formed.

I am still by nature lethargic and placid. I could still occupy myself contentedly With bricks and soldiers, art and history, and trouble no one. But there is still that other element, instilled by Hugh—a love of the open air, of struggle with the elements, in lonely desert places.

I have never lost the craving for true religion, which induced my mother to go to a poor church to worship, and to visit the drunken and helpless in their slums. I have never lost the desire for her singleness of mind, and simple loyalty to Christ and His Church. At the same time I have never lost my father's inquiring spirit,broad view, love of doctrine tempered by reason and founded on history and tested by human experience. When these two beloved ones passed from this world I learnt the meaning of the text, "Where your treasure is, there will your heart be also." My heart has never been wholly in this world.

So, too, I have always been a man of few friends. Ronnie has had many successors; but seldom more than one at a time. I have never cared much for society. My father and mother neither of them attached much importance to conventions, or to the fictitious values which society puts on clothes or money or position. I have always looked rather for some one to admire, some one whose ideals and personality were congenial, whatever their position or occupation. I have also, on the whole, always preferred comfort to show, simple to elaborate living. This I trace to the simple comfort and naturalness of my old home.

Footnote 3:

"A Student" left a great deal of manuscript, among which this fragment of autobiography is not the least interesting.

CHAPTER II. SCHOOL

I went to a day school kept by Ronnie's father when I was nine. At least, it was a day school for me; but nearly all the boys were boarders. I worked fairly hard, and got prizes. I was fairly good at cricket, and not much good at football. I had only one friend—Ronnie—and about two enemies, both of whom were day boys, and whom I should have liked to have fought if I had dared. My memories of the school are few. I best remember leaving home, and going back, and also playing cricket. Ronnie's father lives as a just and straightforward gentleman, who never caned a boy except for what was mean or dirty, and whom we allloved and respected. But then I have known and loved him and his wife all my life. If our house was a second home to Ronnie, theirs has always been a second home to me.

There was one master whom I liked, and who perhaps did something to develop my character. He was fond of poetry and history, and from him I learnt—an easy lesson for me—to love history; but what is more, he first gave me a glimmering idea, which was to develop long after, that the classics are literature, and not torture.

I left there to go to Rugby.

Never did a boy enter Rugby with better chances. The memory of my three brothers still lived in the house. They had all achieved distinction in games, and been leading prefects (or sixths as they are called at Rugby) in the house. Many masters remembered them for good, particularly Jacky, the housemaster, who had loved them all, especially Hugh.

In addition to this, one of the leading fellows in the house, who was afterwards to be captain of the school fifteen and cricket eleven, lieutenant in the corps, and one of the racquet pair, had been at my private school. I shared a study with another fellow who had been at my private school. Two boys accompanied me from there, one of whom was my next best friend to

Ronnie. His parents were in India, and he had spent some of his holidays with Ronnie and me.

But though I loved Rugby and was happy there, I can't say I was a success. I made few friends, who have since, with one exception, drifted out of my life. I was too timid to enjoy Rugger. I never achieved distinction at cricket. I got into the sixth my last term, but hadn't the force of character to enjoy the prefectural powers which that fact conferred upon me. The fact is that I left when I was 16, and it is between 16 and 18 that thefull enjoyment of school life comes and boys reap the harvest they have sown. Had I stayed another year I should have belonged to the leading generation, strengthened my friendships and developed what was latent in my character. As it was, I left at an unfortunate age. I was pushed into the sixth a year before my contemporaries. My friendships were only half formed, and I had only just begun to feel strength of body and mind developing in me.

As a junior I was too conscientious, and not light-hearted enough. I hardly had any adventures at Rugby, because I had an incurable instinct for keeping rules. I worked hard at mathematics and French, and my report generally read, "Good ability. Might exert himself more." At classics and chemistry I did as little work as possible, and any report generally read, "Hard-working but not bright."

On the whole I think I was pretty happy at Rugby; but I never look back to myschool days as the happiest part of my life. I have had many happier times since. But still, my house was a good one. Jacky, the housemaster, was wonderfully kind and wise. He hardly ever interfered with the affairs of the house, but left it all—in appearance—to the "Sixths." Actually, nothing escaped him. The tone of the house was on the whole extraordinarily clean and wholesome, and the fellows who had dirty minds were a small minority, and easily avoided. At all events, very little of that sort of thing reached me.

At sixteen and a half I went to the Royal Military Academy at Woolwich, commonly known as "the Shop." There I spent the two most miserable years of my life, and made the second of my great friendships. In these days the Shop was still a pretty rough place, and at the moment it was unusually full. I think there were over 300 fellows there altogether, and there were about 70 in my term. My firstexperience was unfortunate. I was interviewing the Adjutant, a keen sportsman and a bit of a tartar. He eyed me unfavourably, asked what games I could play, and when I replied that I had no great proficiency in any he commented, "Humph, a good-for-nothing!" and dismissed me.

I am by nature slow, stolid and clumsy. I was bad at being "smart"; I was slow and clumsy at drill; map making and geometrical drawing were physical impossibilities to me; I was incredibly slow and stupid at machinery, mechanism and electricity. The only subject which interested me was military history. In my first term I dropped from about forty-fourth to about seventieth in my class, and I kept near the bottom until my fourth term, when I failed in my electricity exam., and had to stay one term more. In the same term I received a prize for the best essay on the lessons of the South African War.

Oh, the misery of those terms at Woolwich! I hated the work, the drill, the gym and even the riding school. I hated the officers, and above all I hated the spirit of the place. As far as I remember, the one eternal topic of conversation and subject of "wit" was the sexual relation. Of course the boys had never been taught sensibly anything about it. Consequently the place was continually circulated with filthy books, pictures, stories, etc. When I went there I was extraordinarily innocent, and devoid of curiosity. I had been recently the more disposed to purity through the death of my mother. At Woolwich I remained extraordinarily innocent and uncurious, letting the poisonous stream flow continually by me, shrinking from its stench, and finding more and more relief in my own company. I must have been a very unpleasant person at that time.

One friend I had. He was a small, compact, keen, and capable little Rugbiannamed F———. He was like me in that he had recently lost his parents, and was interested in religion and philosophy in a boyish way. Unlike me he rather enjoyed Woolwich. He had a lot of friends, was keen on riding and on a good deal of the work, and generally speaking plunged into life, taking the rough with the smooth, and both in good part. Although we have drifted far apart in ideals and sympathies, and though misunderstanding has come in and destroyed our friendship, I shall never cease to be grateful for all that F——— did for me in those days. He routed me out when I was in the blues, laughed at me, cheered me up and made me look at life with new eyes. Moreover he did this, as I know, in defiance of the set with whom he was friendly, who despised me for a milksop, and were at no pains to conceal the fact. But for F———, my life at the Shop would have been intolerable.

Besides him, I had a few associates,boys with whom I naturally associated for the simple reason that they, too, were left out of the main current of the life of the place. But they were not particularly congenial. One or two were hard workers. One was a great slacker, and more timid, physically and morally, than even I. He was a boy with a fatal facility for doing useless things moderately well, especially in the musical line. He was even more frightened of gym and horses than I was, and unlike me was not ashamed to show it. If the Shop was purgatory to me, it must have been hell to him.

My happiest times were week-ends spent at home. I used to arrive on Saturday evening and leave on Sunday evening. About now I began to get to know my father much better, and to develop my theological bent under his advice. In my disillusionment as to my capacity for military life I began to wish I had chosen the clerical profession. I thinkmy father had the shrewdness to see that failure in one profession was not necessarily the sign of a "call" in another direction. Anyway, he did not discourage me; but spoke of five years in the Army as the best training for a parson.

I remember avowing my intention of becoming a parson to one of my more friendly acquaintances at the Shop, and he replied that I wouldn't set the Thames on fire, because I had such a monotonous voice.

In spite of seeking relief from my uncongenial surroundings in religion and theology, I did not join myself to any one else. There was a so-called "Pi Squad," or Bible class, held weekly, but I only went once, and didn't like it. I was always peculiarly sensitive about priggishness in those who professed themselves to be religious openly, and generally thought I detected priggishness in any "Bible circle" or similar institution that I came across. I think my theologymainly consisted in speculations about the future state—I remember I emphatically declined to believe in hell—and my religion consisted mainly in fairly regular attendance at Matins and Communion.

Another effect of the intensity with which I hated my surroundings was that I read a lot of good novels—George Eliot, the Brontës, Scott, Dickens, Jane Austen, Thackeray, Besant, etc. A book which I read over and over again was Arthur Benson's Hill of Trouble, and other Stories. Those legends, with their imaginative setting, charm of language and beautiful religious ideas were more restful to my unquiet spirit than anything else I read.

The actual conditions of life at the Shop were pretty barbaric. The aim was to make it as much like barracks as possible. Each term was housed in a different side of the square of buildings which form the Academy, and the fourth term were spread among the houses of the other terms ascorporals. My first term I shared a room with three other fellows. I think it was the ugliest room I have ever lived in, without exception. It had high whitewashed brick walls. In each corner was a bed which folded up against the wall in the day time, and was concealed by a square of print curtains. There were a deal table, four windsor chairs, a shelf with four basins, and a cupboard with four lockers. All the woodwork was painted khaki. The contrast with the little study at Rugby, with its diamond-paned window, its matchboard panelling surmounted by a paper of one's own choosing, its ledge for photos and ornaments ("bim ledge" so called), its eggshell blue cupboards, baize curtains and window box, was striking.

It used to be the custom to go to and from the bathroom attired in a sponge, in connexion with which an amusing incident once happened.

A cadet in his second year was on thebathroom landing, when he perceived that the mother and sisters of another cadet were coming upstairs. From sounds in the bathroom he realized that they would meet a naked corporal just as they reached the landing. The door of the bathroom opened outwards, and with admirable presence of mind he rushed back, and putting his back against the door and his feet against the wall, imprisoned the corporal. The corporal, in the approved Shop version of Billingsgate, began to blaspheme at the top of his voice, so when the ladies reached the top of the stairs they saw a vision of a cadet with his feet to the wall and his back to a door singing at the top of his voice to drown a Commotion within!

On another occasion in my second year, when I was sharing a room with one other fellow, I had a sister to tea. On arriving in my room I found that my stablemate had been playing hockey, and was at the moment in the bathroom, having thoughtlesslyleft all his clothes in the room—mostly on the floor.

On the last day of my first term the corporals and officers were all absent at a farewell dinner to the former, and we received information that the third term were going to raid our house, with a view to "toshing" us in a cold bath. We therefore prepared for action. Every receptacle which would hold water was taken to the upper landing, full. Then all the chairs in the house were roped together, and placed on the stairs as an obstacle. The defenders then took up their position at the windows and at the top of the stairs. In due course the enemy's forces arrived, and stormed the stairs, under a heavy fire of water. The obstacle was at length destroyed, and a solid phalanx of wet bodies swarmed up the stairs. We formed a similar phalanx and charged to meet them. I happened to be first, and much to my discomfiturethe enemy's phalanx parted in the middle, and I was rapidly passed down the stairs—a prisoner! Fortunately at the bottom I found a relieving party from the next house, making a diversion on the enemy's rear. With great valour we dragged down a foe, and toshed him in the bath that had been made ready for us. "The tosher toshed!"

The next day we surveyed the damage. All the chairs and banisters were broken, the whitewash was rubbed off the bricks by wet shoulders and nearly all the basins were broken. That day was the day of Lord Roberts's half-yearly inspection!

There was not such another battle until my third term, when we were the aggressors. This time the damage was even greater, for the defenders let down tables across the stairs as an obstacle, and we battered our way through with scaffolding poles. There were some casualties that day, owing to an indiscriminate use of mop handles.

On the day of Lord Roberts's inspection we had to change from parade dress to gym dress, and it was during the change that Lord Roberts inspected our quarters. He went into one room and found a fellow just half-way through his change—with nothing at all on! The room was called to attention, and with great presence of mind the boy dashed into the bed curtains and stood to attention there, while Lord Roberts had an animated conversation with him!

There were jolly moments in the life at the Shop. On Saturdays, after dinner, the unfortunates who had not got away for the week-end used to have "stodges" after dinner. Having put away a substantial dinner, we changed into flannels, and used to crowd into some one's room, and eat muffins and smoke cigars. I remember one night there were eighteen of us in one small room.

In order to go away for a week-end onehad to obtain (1) an invitation, (2) permission from parent or guardian to accept the invitation. One week my brother, who was working at the Admiralty, offered his flat to myself and F——, as he was going to Brighton himself. Fleming wrote to his guardian—a Scotsman—for permission to stay with Captain Hankey. The guardian wrote back for more information. He saw by the Army List that Captain Hankey existed, but who were the Hankeys? etc., etc. F—— wrote back a furious letter, saying that he expected to have his friends accepted without question, and received the permission. We went. The awkward thing was that Captain Hankey was not there, and we shuddered to think of the rage of F——'s guardian if he should find out. Worse still, the guardian was supposed to be staying at the Oriental Club in Hanover Square, and my brother's flat was in Oxford Street! However, we didn't meet.

F—— and I neither of us knew London, and had the time of our lives. We dined at Frascati's—a palace of splendour in our eyes—and went to His Majesty's to see Beerbohm Tree in Ulysses. When it came to Hades, we held each other's hands! On Sunday we went to St. Peter's, Vere Street, but were so furious at being kept waiting for pew holders long after service had commenced, that we went on to the Audley Street Chapel, a most queer little place. It was full of monuments to the dependents of peers, in which the peers figured very largely and the dependents fared humbly—the epitome of flunkeydom. Among these tablets was one inscribed—

"To John Wilkes,
Friend of Liberty."
Truly refreshing!

We finished the day at some old friends of mine, and voted the week-end a huge success.

When I went to Woolwich I was just on the verge of getting keen on games and beginning to feel self-confident, and to enjoy the fellowship of my comrades. Woolwich nipped this in the bud. I left with no self-confidence, having renounced games, and with a sense of solitariness among my comrades. I was a misanthrope, and the unhappiest sort of egotist—the kind that dislikes himself. To say the truth, too, I was then, and always have been, a bit of a funk, physically, which didn't make me happier. On the other hand, I was an omnivorous reader of everything which did not concern my profession, and a dabbler in military history.

I have sometimes thought that I was unconsciously a bit of a hero at Woolwich, standing out for purity and religion in an atmosphere of filth

A STUDENT IN ARMS

and blasphemy. I have come to the conclusion, however, that there was nothing in this. As to the general atmosphere, there is no doubt that it wassingularly pernicious; even the officers and instructors contributed their quota of filthy jokes, and there was no religious instruction or influence at all except the parade service at the garrison church on Sunday, if one happened not to be on leave. But as to my heroism I am reluctantly compelled to be sceptical. I went as far as I felt my inclination, and stopped after a time because instinct was too strong the other way.

As I have said before, I have always had an insurmountable instinct for keeping rules. At school I could never bring myself to transgress, although I knew that transgression was the road to adventure. So at the Shop, however much I may have wished to be in the swim, my instinct for the moral and religious code of home was too strong for me. It required no self-control to prevent myself from slipping into blasphemy and filth. On the contrary, in order to do so I should have had to violate my strongest instincts, and exercised awill to evil much stronger than any will power that I possessed at that time. If, when I left Woolwich, I was comparatively pure, it was because nature did not allow me to be anything else.

To say the truth, I have never felt the sway of passions to anything like the same extent as most men seem to. I have never cared for the society of women for its sexual attraction. Consequently all my women friends have been just the same to me as my men friends—friends whom I could talk to about the things that interested me.

I don't boast of this, I only state the fact. I am not proud of it because I know that some passion is necessary to make heroes and even saints.

SOME NOTES ON THE FRAGMENT OF AUTOBIOGRAPHY BY HILDA

I have before me as I write a pencil sketch, limned with considerable care, of a rather disagreeable looking young man, and beneath it is written—"D.W.A.H., by Himself."

It is a profile. The eye has almost disappeared under the brow, the mouth is tightly closed to a degree that is quite unpleasant and there is a deliberate exaggeration of a slight defect he actually had—a tendency for the lower jaw to protrude a little. This little defect hardly any of his friends seem to have noticed, for most of them execrate it as a libel in the otherwise admittedly beautiful photograph at the beginning of this volume. The expression in the sketch is above all—dubious.

So did Donald see himself.

For the rest of us no doubt the lessons Mr. Haselden has for us in his caricatures, "ourselves as we see ourselves" and "as others see us," are necessary. But not for Donald. The drawing is pasted into an album which contains mainly Oxford College groups, and there is a certain unpleasant resemblance between it and his full face presentment in one of the groups—in which he has "the group expression" rather badly. Assuming it to have been drawn at Oxford, or not very long after he left, I think it must belong very nearly to a time when he was going off abroad on one of his long trips, and I had the sympathy of a dear old lady friend of ours on having to part with him. I remember replying, "Yes, it always seems as if peace and happiness, truth and justice, religion and piety went with him when he goes!" She laughed a good deal, and then said, seriously, repeating over to herself the stately mounting sixteenth century phrases, "But it's quite true, you know!" I hardly think, though, that I should have said it of

DONALD HANKEY

the young man in the sketch!

I am now going to make a comment ortwo on my brother's word-pictures as I should if he were by my side. But first I should like his readers to know and realize that both were written before the period of what I may call Donald's "Renaissance," a period that can be roughly marked by the publication of his first book, The Lord of all Good Life.

Up to then he had been struggling in vain for self-expression. How he had worked the amount of MSS. he has left alone proves—for we have it on a friend's testimony that "he tore up much of what he wrote"; and he also had experienced and suffered, violating his natural "timidity" and his in some ways, precarious health, for he had never got over certain weaknesses engendered by his illness in Mauritius—in his struggle to get a true basis for a solution of the meaning of life and of religion. What cost him most was the knowledge that he was frequently doubted and misunderstood by many of those whose approbation would have been very dear to him. This is proved by his constantly expressed gratitude to the one or two who never doubted him for one moment.

With the writing of this book, as we know, all his difficulties began to clear away, and at the same time he began to reap the harvest of love and admiration that he had sown in his toils to produce it. And the result was he opened out like a flower to the sun! No one can doubt this for a moment who has read his book of a year later, The Student in Arms, and rejoiced in the radiant happiness of its inspiration.

He had more than once said to me during the past two years, "You know it makes a tremendous difference to me when people really like me." No longer was it a case of "one friend at a time." The period for that was over and done with. He had come into his own. He was ready for a universal brotherhood, and no hand would ever be held out to him in vain.

It is impossible to believe that he does not now know of and appreciate all the beautiful tributes that have come to him since his "passing"—from the perfect wreath of immortelles weaved by Mr. Strachey to the sweet pansy of thought dropped by a little fellow V.A.D. of minewho said beautifully and courageously—though knowing him solely through his book—"We feel since he gave us his thought that he belongs a tiny bit to us, too," thus voicing the feeling of many.

I believe the paper entitled "My Home" to have been written at Oxford, and "School" not so very long after. In any case, I have definite proof of their both belonging to Donald's pre-"Renaissance" period, for the friendship with F——, that began at "the Shop" and went under a cloud for a time, was renewed with fresh vigour in 1914, and has burned brightly ever since. Only last July was I sent by him a letter of F——'s from the trenches, with the injunction, "Please put this among my treasures," and there is an allusion to a story told in this letter in the article entitled "Romance" of the

A STUDENT IN ARMS

present volume.

To return to "My Home," I question whether the love and devotion of "Hilda" and "Ma" for Hugh was so entirely unselfish. For my mother I fully believe, as for "Hilda," Hugh was the epitome of all that was fine, splendid and joyous in life. He was the glorious knight, the "preuxchevalier" "sans peur et sans reproche," who rode forth at dawn with clean sword and shining armour, and all the world before him, yet keeping his heart for ever in his home. He was the child of her youth as Donald was the child of her maturity. Deep down in her wonderfully varied nature there were certain bottomless springs of courage, daring and enterprise which she herself had little chance of expressing and of which Hugh alone was the personification.

As long as I can remember Hugh had been my ideal and made all the interest and joy of life for me. Whether he were at home or abroad I never had a thought I did not share with him. When he died, the best part of me died too, or was paralysed rather, and Heaven knows what sort of a "substitute" I should have been for "Ma" to Donald, had not the baby Hugh come, just in time, with healing in his wings to restore life to the best part of me!

I am glad to think that Donald's "Autobiography" was written before 1914, for I know that even before that I was becoming more to him than a "substitute." I too have my memories and pictures!

It is May, 1915. I am in the country-house—cleaning is going on at home.

I get a letter to say that the Rifle Brigade may leave for France at any time, and that Donald may get some "leave" on Saturday or Sunday.

I make a dash for town.

There I find a telegram of reckless and unconscionable length, running into two pages. He cannot come up—they may leave at any moment. It seems hardly worth while my bothering to come to Aldershot on the chance—he may be unable to leave barracks.

I write a return telegram—also of reckless and unconscionable length, and reply paid—it is a relief to do so—asking for a place of meeting at Aldershot to be suggested.

I get no answer at all, and on Sunday morning, in despair, I go over to see my aunt and cousin. My aunt is my mother's sister and a sportswoman. She counsels, "Go at all costs." Dorothy will come with me: Dorothy is Donald's best woman pal—she reminds him of his mother. She is all that is wholesome and comportable.

The element of enjoyment comes in, and I go home and pack a nice lunch.

We arrive at Aldershot.

There is no one on the platform to meet us, and we push our way through the turnstile.

There is Donald, on the outskirts of the waiting crowd—a tall, soldierly

DONALD HANKEY

figure in the uniform of a private—for he has resigned his sergeant's stripes by now.

His face is very boyish—not the face of the photograph at the beginning of this book: that was taken after he had been to France, and had been wounded, and had written "A Passing in June," and "The Honour of the Brigade"—but a much younger face, really boyish.

He glances quickly and anxiously at every face that passes, and each time he is a little more disappointed—but he tries not to show it.

I am not tall and cannot catch his eye. It is like being at a play, watching him! All at once he sees me! Involuntarily a sudden quick spasm of joy passes across his face, absolutely transfiguring it.

He smooths it away quickly, for he is aBriton and does not like to show his feelings—but he has given himself away!

Dorothy and I shall never forget that look. And it was for me—at first he does not see Dorothy. When he does it is an added pleasure.

With two ladies to escort he assumes a lordly air.

He had thought of everything. We would like some tea? Yes, all the big places are shut as it is Sunday, but he has marked down a little place on his way to the station.

It is a lovely day, and we are very happy!

The girl who waits upon us at the little tea place likes us, and so do the other Tommies and their friends who are having tea there.

We sit at little tables, but at very close quarters with each other, and we smile at them and they at us.

I have brought Donald some letters, which pleases him, and Dorothy has brought him some splendid socks, knitted by herself.

After tea we walk across an arid plain to a little wood, and sit down under the trees.

Donald changes to the new socks—those he had on were wringing wet!

He picks us little bunches of violets, hyacinths and wild strawberry flowers—we have them still.

We are very happy the whole of the day, and have my sandwiches and cake and fruit for supper, there under the trees. And here in thought let me leave "The Student in Arms," who was to me part son, best pal, brother, comrade, and counsellor on all subjects—and more than a little bit of grandpapa!

He could be so many different things because, as another friend and cousin said, "he seemed to know everything about everybody."

I like to think of those two fine spirits—Hugh and Donald—each with a hand to the tiny baby nephew, and a word of greeting for me when I go over the top.

THE END

A STUDENT IN ARMS

Printed in Great Britain
by Amazon